THE HERITAGE OF INDIA

THE SAMKHYA SYSTEM

THE HERITAGE OF INDIA

THE

SAMKHYA SYSTEM

A History of the Samkhya Philosophy

By

A. BERRIEDALE KEITH, D.C.L., D. LITT.

GYAN

Published by

GYAN

Gyan Publishing House
5, Ansari Road
Daryaganj, New Delhi-110002
Phone: 011-47034999, 9811692060
E-mail: books@gyanbooks.com

Distribution Network
gyanbooks.com
India, USA, Canada, UK, Australia, France

ISBN : 978-81-212-6625-3 (PB)
First Published, 1918

2nd Impression 2022

Printed at: Gyan Press, Delhi.

THE HERITAGE OF INDIA THE SAMKHYA SYSTEM
Author: A. BERRIEDALE KEITH

THE HERITAGE OF INDIA

Joint Editors. { The Right Reverend V. S. AZARIAH, Bishop of Dornakal.
J. N. FARQUHAR, M.A., D.LITT. (Oxon.).

Already published.

The Heart of Buddhism. K. J. SAUNDERS, M.A.
Asoka. REV. J. M. MACPHAIL, M.A., M.D.
Indian Painting. Principal PERCY BROWN, Calcutta.
Kanarese Literature. REV. E. P. RICE, B.A.

Subjects proposed and volumes under preparation.

SANSKRIT AND PALI LITERATURE.

Hymns from the Vedas. Prof. A. A. MACDONELL, Oxford.
Anthology of Mahāyāna Literature. Prof. L. DE LA VALLEE POUSSIN, Ghent.
Selections from the Upanishads. F. J. WESTERN, M.A., Delhi.
Scenes from the Rāmāyaṇa. JAMES MORISON, M.A., PH.D., Oxford.
Selections from the Mahābhārata.

THE PHILOSOPHIES.

The Philosophy of the Upanishads.
Śaṇkara's Vedānta. A. K. SHARMA, M.A., Patiala.
Rāmānuja's Vedānta.
The Buddhist System.

FINE ART AND MUSIC.

Indian Architecture. R. L. EWING, B.A., Madras.
Indian Sculpture. Principal W. M. ZUMBRO, Madura.

Indian Music. H. A. Popley, B.A., Erode.

The Minor Arts. Principal Percy Brown, Calcutta.

Indian Coins.

BIOGRAPHIES OF EMINENT INDIANS.

Gautama Buddha. K. J. Saunders, M.A., Rangoon.

Rāmānuja.

Akbar. F. V. Slack, M.A., Calcutta.

Tulsī Dās. S. K. Dutta, B.A., M.B., Ch.B., Lahore.

VERNACULAR LITERATURE.

The Kurral. H. A. Popley, B.A., Erode.

Hymns of the Aḍiyārs. G. E. Phillips, M.A., and Francis Kingsbury, Bangalore.

Hymns of the Āḷvārs.

Tāyumānavar. Isaac Tambyah, M.A., Bar.-at-Law, Penang.

Hymns of Hindustān.

Chaitanya Hymns. O. Stursberg, Ph.D., Berhampore, Murshidabad.

Marāṭhī Abhangs. Nicol Macnicol, M.A., D.Litt., Poona.

Gujarātī Hymns.

HISTORIES OF VERNACULAR LITERATURE.

Bengālī. J. D. Anderson, Cambridge.

Gujarātī.

Hindī. Edwin Greaves, Benares.

Marāṭhī. Nicol Macnicol, M.A., D.Litt., Poona.

Tamil. Francis Kingsbury, Bangalore.

Telugu.

Sinhalese. H. S. Perera, B.A., Kandy.

EDITORIAL PREFACE

> Finally, brethren, whatsoever things are true, whatsoever things are honourable, whatsoever things are just, whatsoever things are pure, whatsoever things are lovely, whatsoever things are of good report; if there be any virtue, and if there be any praise, think on these things.

No section of the population of India can afford to neglect her ancient heritage. In her literature, philosophy, art, and regulated life there is much that is worthless, much also that is distinctly unhealthy; yet the treasures of knowledge, wisdom, and beauty which they contain are too precious to be lost. Every citizen of India needs to use them, if he is to be a cultured modern Indian. This is as true of the Christian, the Muslim, the Zoroastrian as of the Hindu. But, while the heritage of India has been largely explored by scholars, and the results of their toil are laid out for us in their books, they cannot be said to be really available for the ordinary man. The volumes are in most cases expensive, and are often technical and difficult. Hence this series of cheap books has been planned by a group of Christian men, in order that every educated Indian, whether rich or poor, may be able to find his way into the treasures of India's past. Many Europeans, both in India and elsewhere, will doubtless be glad to use the series.

The utmost care is being taken by the General Editors in selecting writers, and in passing manuscripts for the press. To every book two tests are rigidly applied: everything must be scholarly, and everything must be sympathetic. The purpose is to bring the best out of the ancient treasuries, so that it may be known, enjoyed, and used.

I.

THE SĀṀKHYA IN THE UPANIṢADS

In all the manifold character of the content of the Upaniṣads it is undoubtedly possible to trace certain leading ideas. The most important of these doctrines is, beyond question, that of the identity of the self, Ātman, of the individual with the Brahman, which is the most universal expression for the absolute in which the universe finds its unity. It is probable enough that these two expressions are not intrinsically related, and that they represent two different streams of thought.* The Brahman is the devotion of the Brāhman priest: it is the sacred hymn to propitiate the gods: it is also the magic spell of the wonder-worker: more generally it is the holy power in the universe at least as much as it is the magic fluid of primitive savagery. Religion and magic, if different in essence and in origin, nevertheless go often in closest alliance, and their unison in the case of the concept Brahman may explain the ease with which that term came to denote the essence of the universe or absolute being. The Ātman, on the other hand, in the Brāhmaṇa texts which lie before the Upaniṣads, has very often the sense of the trunk of the body, as opposed to the hands and feet and other members, and it is perhaps from that fact at least as much as from the fact that it has also the sense of wind that it develops into the meaning of the essential self of man. The identification of the self and the Brahman results in one form of the doctrine of the Upaniṣads, that taught under the name of Yājñavalkya in

* See H. Oldenberg, *Buddha* (5th ed.), pp. 30-33; P. Deussen (*Philosophy of the Upaniṣads*, p. 39) prefers to treat Brahman as the cosmical and Ātman as the psychical principle of unity. Max Müller (*Six Systems of Indian Philosophy*, pp. 68-93) distinguishes Brahman, speech, and Brahman as that which utters or drives forth or manifests or creates.

the *Bṛhadāraṇyaka Upaniṣad* (ii, 4; iv, 5), in the conclusion that the Ātman as the knowing subject is unknowable, and that the world of empiric reality, which seems to be in constant change, is really a mere illusion. This is the highest point reached by the thought of the Upaniṣads, and it is not consistently or regularly maintained. Despite acceptance of the doctrine of the identity of the individual self and the self of the universe, there often appears to be left over as an irreducible element something which is not the self, but which is essentially involved in the constitution of reality. This is implicit in such statements as that the Ātman completely enters into the body, up to the nails even: the all-pervasiveness of the Ātman is not incompatible with the existence of something to be pervaded. In order to remove the difficulty which is felt in the existence of this further element, the conception of creation, which was, of course, familiar from the cosmogonic legends of the Brāhmaṇas, was often resorted to. Thus in the *Chāndogya Upaniṣad* (vi, 2) we learn in detail how the self desired to be many and created brilliance, Tejas, whence arose water and food, and then the self entered into these created things with the living self. This scheme, by which a being first produces a cosmic material and then enters into it as life, is a commonplace in the speculations of the Brāhmaṇas, and it lends itself to a very different development than the theory of illusion. While the latter theory insists on the identity of the individual self with the absolute self, both being one essence surpassing all consciousness, the latter system allows a certain reality to matter, and a still more definite reality to the individual soul, which in course of time develops into the doctrine of qualified duality, Viśiṣṭādvaita, in which there is found a place for the individual soul and matter beside the supreme soul, and which undoubtedly forms the theme of the *Brahma Sūtra* of Bādarāyaṇa. But while this system can be seen in the Upaniṣads, it would be an error to suppose that it is more properly the doctrine of the Upaniṣads than the illusion theory of Śaṁkara:* neither

* For Bādarāyaṇa's views see Thibaut, *S.B.E.*, xxiv; Sukhtankar, *Vienna Oriental Journal*, xii, 120 ff,; H. Jacobi, *J.A.O.S.*, xxxiii, 51-54.

system in its completely self-conscious form is to be found in the Upaniṣads, but the germs of both are present, and both in a real sense can claim the authority of the Upaniṣads.

On the other hand, it is impossible to find in the Upaniṣads any real basis for the Sāṁkhya system. The Upaniṣads are essentially devoted to the discovery of an absolute, and, diverse as are the forms which the absolute may take, they do not abandon the search, nor do they allow that no such absolute exists. There are, however, elements here and there which mark the growth of ideas which later were thrown into systematic form in the Sāṁkhya, but it is impossible to see in these fragmentary hints any indication that the Sāṁkhya philosophy was then in process of formation. It is, of course, possible, as a matter of abstract argument, to insist that the elements in the Upaniṣads which suggest the later Sāṁkhya views are really borrowings by the Upaniṣads of doctrines already extant in a Sāṁkhya system, but, in the absense of the slightest evidence for the existence of such a system in the Vedic literature, it is methodologically unsound to take this hypothesis as possessing any value, in face of the natural conclusion that we have in the Upaniṣads scattered hints which were later amalgamated into one system. Just like the Vedānta of Śaṁkara, or the Vedānta of Bādarāyaṇa, the Sāṁkhya is a system built on the Upaniṣads: from both of these it differs in that it goes radically and essentially beyond the teaching of the Upaniṣads.

The cosmogonical form of the doctrine of the self sets at once the absolute into conflict with the individual self, and it undoubtedly tends to minimise the importance of the absolute, since its operation appears to have been exhausted by the action of creation. At the same time, it is clear that the opposition of matter to the individual soul becomes quite a sharp one, for on the cosmogonic or theistic system the primitive matter is indeed produced from the absolute, but equally clearly it exists before the individual soul enters into the sphere of existence. While thus the relation of soul and nature becomes one of opposition under the aegis of an absolute which tends to become more faded, at the same time reflection is more bent on the actual character of the relation of soul and nature, and finds expression in such an utterance as that of the *Bṛhadāraṇyaka Upaniṣad* (i, 4, 6), where it is expressly stated that food and eater make up the entire universe. This passage is interpreted in the late *Maitrāyaṇī Upaniṣad* as referring to the distinction between spirit, which is subject, and all the rest of nature, including the Bhūtātman, the psychic apparatus produced from nature, as the object: it is characteristic of the confused character of this late work that the very next chapters (vi, 11-13) deal with nature as being the product of the supreme Brahman. It would be wrong, therefore, to find in the *Bṛhadāraṇyaka Upaniṣad* any conscious realization of a doctrine which would eliminate the Brahman, but it is clear enough that the path to the elimination of that element was open.

The denial in the Sāṁkhya of the supreme spirit carries with it curious consequences when added to the extreme development of the doctrine that the spirit is alone the subject. The first product of nature is the intellect, which is called the great one, and which clearly is originally a cosmic function, derived from nature but lighted up by spirit. The natural source of this conception must be found in the idea in the Upaniṣads that the supreme spirit reappears as the firstborn of creation after it has produced the primitive matter. The ultimate origin of the idea can be traced beyond the Upaniṣads to the *Ṛgveda* (x, 121) where the golden germ Hiraṇyagarbha is produced from the primeval waters, and in the Upaniṣads we find in the *Kauṣītaki* the seer, composed of the Brahman, the great one in the *Kaṭha* (iii, 10, 13; vi, 7), the first great spirit in the *Śvetāśvatara* (ii, 19) who is called Hiraṇyagarbha in iii, 4; iv, 12; Brahman in vi, 18, and the knower, all-pervading, in vi, 17. Moreover, it is thus that we should, it is clear, understand the seer, Kapila, first engendered, in v, 2. The idea that in this verse we are to see the first mention of the founder of the Sāṁkhya as a real person is too fantastic to be seriously upheld, though it is not at all unlikely that the origin of the doctrine of Kapila as the founder of Sāṁkhya is to be traced to this passage.

THE HERITAGE OF INDIA

THE SĀṀKHYA SYSTEM

A History of the Samkhya Philosophy

BY

A. BERRIEDALE KEITH, D.C.L., D.LITT.

OF THE INNER TEMPLE BARRISTER-AT-LAW, REGIUS PROFESSOR OF SANSKRIT AND COMPARATIVE PHILOLOGY AT THE UNIVERSITY OF EDINBURGH.

TRANSLATOR OF THE TAITTIRIYA SAMHITA, ETC.

CONTENTS

PAGE

I. SAMKHYA IN THE UPANIṢADS 5

II. SAMKHYA AND BUDDHISM 20

III. THE PHILOSOPHY OF THE GREAT EPIC AND THE ORIGIN OF SAMKHYA 29

IV SAMKHYA AND YOGA 54

V. THE ṢAṢTITANTRA 59

VI. GREEK PHILOSOPHY AND THE SAMKHYA 65

VII. THE SAMKHYA KARIKA 68

VIII. THE LATER SAMKHYA 89

INDEX 105

Further material for the origin of the series of evolution is also to be found in the Upaniṣads. In the *Kaṭha*, which has every claim to be regarded as an old work,* not indeed of the same antiquity as the great prose Upaniṣads like the *Bṛhadāraṇyaka*, *Chāndogya*, *Aitareya*, *Taittirīya*, or *Kauṣītaki*, but at the head of the second stage of poetical Upaniṣads, representing the period of the full development of the philosophy of these texts, there is found (iii, 10-13), after an exhortation to control the unruly steeds of the senses, a description of Yoga, or concentration. In this it is expressly stated that the objects are higher than the senses, mind than the objects, the intellect than mind, the great self than intellect, the unevolved than the great self, and the spirit than the unevolved. The spirit dwells unseen in all beings and is above all. In concentration, therefore, speech with mind is to be restrained in the knowledge-self, that is intellect, that again in the great self, and that in the calm self, that is the unevolved. In a later passage (vi, 7-11) a similar account is given: here the mind stands above the senses, Sattva above the mind, over that the great self, over that the unevolved, over that the spirit which is described by terms applicable in the classical Sāṁkhya, as all-pervading and without any distinctive mark. The highest condition of Yoga is reached when the senses with mind and intellect are brought to a standstill. In the next lines the spirit is described as only to be expressed by the declaration of existence. With this series may be compared the fact that according to the *Chāndogya* (vi, 8, 6) at death speech enters into mind, mind into breath, breath into brilliance and brilliance into the supreme godhead.

Further light is thrown on the position by the *Praśna Upaniṣad*, which, though not a work of the same age as the *Kaṭha*, is nevertheless probably the earliest of the later prose Upaniṣads. In the fourth Praśna it is explained that in sleep in dreaming the senses enter into mind, and in deep sleep mind also passes into the brilliance, Tejas. Then follows an account of how all things are resolved into the

* See H. Oldenberg, *Z.D.M.G.*, xxxvii, 57ff; *Buddha*, p. 60; P. Deussen, *Philosophy of the Upaniṣads*, p. 24.

imperishable, which has no shadow, blood or body, the order being the five elements, each with its corresponding Mātrā, which appears to denote the corresponding fine element, the five organs of perception with their functions, the five organs of action with their functions, the mind, intellect, individuation, Ahaṁkāra, thought, Citta, brilliance, and breath, and their functions. From the highest self there is here distinguished the Vijñānātman, the individual self, which experiences the impressions of the senses, and so forth. It is perfectly clear that the *Praśna* is not an exposition of the Sāṁkhya, but the elements of the Sāṁkhya derivation are present. The conception of the fine elements seems to owe its origin to the view expressed in the *Chāndogya Upaniṣad* (vi, 3), according to which the gross elements, corresponding to fire, water and earth, are not in themselves pure, but each is compounded with some portion of the others: the name, Tanmātra, which is later normal, is first given expressly in the *Maitrāyaṇī Upaniṣad* (iii, 2).

A much more developed account of Sāṁkhya type is to be found in the *Śvetāśvatara Upaniṣad*, which is no doubt older than the *Praśna*, but later than the *Kaṭha*. The Upaniṣad is definitely deistic, Rudra who bears the epithet but not the name, Śiva, being the object of devotion and belief, but at the same time being regarded as the absolute and supreme spirit, rather than as derived from that spirit. On the other hand, the Upaniṣad contains a series of numbers which are best to be explained as referring to enumerations accepted by the Sāṁkhya school: thus in i, 4, the individual self is compared to a wheel with three tyres, sixteen ends, fifty spokes, twenty counter-spokes and six sets of eight. These are interpreted as the three Guṇas, the set of sixteen consisting of the ten organs, mind and the five elements, the fifty psychic states of the classical Sāṁkhya, the ten senses and their objects, and the six sets of the five elements, mind, individuation and intellect; the eight elements of the body, the eight prefections, the eight psychic states which form in the Sāṁkhya an alternative to the fifty, eight gods and eight virtues. The worth of such identifications must be regarded as uncertain, and no conclusive evidence is afforded by them, as plays on numbers are much affected by the

Brahmanical schools. But there is other and much more convincing evidence of the existence of Sāṁkhya views. The individual self, the Vijñānātman or Puruṣa, is described as the power of god enveloped in his own Guṇas, which shows plainly that while the absolute is still the source of all, nevertheless a new element has been introduced in the conception of the Guṇas, through which the absolute becomes the individual soul. A still more distinct proof of the existence of ideas akin to Sāṁkhya is to be seen in iv, 5, in which it is said:

> The one she-goat, red, white, and black,
> Produceth many young, like-formed unto her,
> The one he-goat in love enjoyeth her,
> The other leaveth her whom he hath enjoyed.

The passage is discussed by Śaṁkara, who seeks to see in the three colours a reference to the three colours mentioned in the *Chāndogya Upaniṣad* (vi, 4) as those of the three elements there mentioned, fire, water, and earth, which are produced from the absolute and which are present in all that exists. This view is so far, it would seem, beyond doubt correct: the resemblance in point of the colours is too striking to be an accident. But the passage must obviously also be admitted to have clear traces of what is later the Sāṁkhya doctrine: the imagery of the many he-goats and the relation of enjoyment, followed by relinquishment, is precisely parallel to the similes which are often used in the classical Sāṁkhya to illustrate the relation of spirit and nature. Moreover the she-goat is named Ajā which denotes also the unborn, a fact which exactly coincides with the Sāṁkhya conception that the first principle nature is not a product. The Sāṁkhya conception of the all-pervading character of the Guṇas, which in diverse measure are present in all the products of nature, is as well suited to the description of the progeny of the goat as the view of the *Chāndogya*. It is, therefore, only reasonable to assume that we have here a clear hint of the origin of the doctrine of the Guṇas in the threefold material of the *Chāndogya Upaniṣad*, and there is nothing in this passage, nor in the others where the Guṇas are mentioned (i, 3; v, 7; vi, 3, 11, 16), to suggest that the Guṇas are anything other than elements as in the *Chāndogya.* The names Sattva, Rajas and Tamas do not occur until the *Maitrāyaṇī Upaniṣad* (ii, 5; v, 2). It is not impossible that the subjective side of the Guṇas, which is clearly marked in these names and which certainly prevails in the classical Sāṁkhya, was a development from the conception that the individual self was the result of the envelopment of the absolute in the three Guṇas: though originally referring to material products, still the tendency would be to see in them psychic states.

It is most probable that in these traces of Sāṁkhya views we are not to see the result of a contamination of Sāṁkhya with a Vedānta philosophy: it is perfectly plain that in iv, 5 we are not dealing with the conscious expression of a view which ignores the absolute; on the contrary in iv, 10 we find the deliberate description of nature as an illusion, and the great lord as an illusion-maker, emphatic denials of the possibility of the separate and real existence of nature as held by the Sāṁkhya school. It is not natural that one who is opposed so essentially to the view that the Sāṁkhya principles are correct should appropriate phrases which seem to accept them, whereas all is natural if we assume that the Upaniṣad represents a definite development of the doctrine of the Absolute based on the older Upaniṣads, from which in due course the Sāṁkhya developed.* With such a view there is nothing inconsistent in iv, 5: the metaphor there used applies perfectly properly to the different condition of two individual souls, the one of which does not realise its true nature as the absolute enveloped in the three Guṇas, while the other recognizes its true nature and throws aside its connection with nature.

It has, however, been argued from the occurrence of the name, Kapila, in v, 2, and of Sāṁkhya in vi, 13, in connection with Yoga, that the Sāṁkhya-Yoga system was definitely known to the author or redactor of the Upaniṣad. But this is clearly not shown by the facts adduced. Kapila is, as we have seen, not a human personage at all, and the parallel of i, 3,

* This is the amount of truth, in the view of A. E. Gough (*Philosophy of the Upaniṣads*, pp. 200, 212), that the Sāṁkhya is originally an enumeration of principles of the Vedānta. No such Sāṁkhya system is recorded, however; as a system Sāṁkhya is atheistic.

where in place of Sāṁkhya and Yoga are found Dhyāna and Yoga, show clearly that we have here Sāṁkhya in the simple sense of meditation as opposed to devotion in Yoga.

The view that the *Śvetāśvatara Upaniṣad* does not contain any reference to an atheistic Sāṁkhya, but merely unites ideas which afterwards are developed in that system, is confirmed by the very different appearance of things in the *Maitrāyaṇī Upaniṣad*, which does contain very clear evidnce of a developed Sāṁkhya belief, and which on the other hand betrays its modern date* by the use of terms such as *sura*, *vigraha*, *nirmama*, *kṣetrajña*, *nāstikya*, and *suṣumṇā*, and even such an expression as *sarvopaniṣadvidyā*, the science of all the Upaniṣads, though a false appearance of archaism has been lent to it by the fact that it preserves, but not faithfully, the archaisms in euphonic combination of words of the *Maitrāyaṇī Saṁhitā* with which it is closely connected. The Upaniṣad clearly reflects a period when various forms of heresy—probably in no small measure the Buddhist—had attacked the main outlines of the system of the Upaniṣads, and it endeavours to restate that position with, as is inevitable, many traits borrowed from the doctrines it was refuting, and among these traits are clear marks of the Sāṁkhya. It is characterized by a profound pessimism which is not countenanced by the older Upaniṣads, which lay no stress normally on that doctrine, but which is characteristic at once of Buddhism and of the Sāṁkhya. Like the *Śvetāśvatara*, it considers that the Brahman is enveloped by Guṇas but these are called the Guṇas of nature and not of itself as in the *Śvetāśvatara*. Through these Guṇas the Brahman falls into the error of individuation and binds itself by itself, a metaphor which in the *Sāṁkhya Kārikā* (63) is transferred to nature herself. In this form there arises the Bhūtātman, which resides in the body composed of the fine and the gross elements, the Tanmātras, and the Mahābhūtas, both of which bear the name of Bhūtas. The highest soul, the individual souls, and the Guṇas are compared with the glow, the iron and the smith, who

* Max Müller (*S.B.E.*, XV, xlvi-lii) argues for an early date, but the evidence against this is conclusively set out by P. Deussen, *Sechzig Upaniṣads*, pp. 311 seq.

hammers only the iron not the glow pervading it. Here, too, we find the names of the Guṇas as psychic states, and bodily and mental evils are referred to the action of Rajas, desire, and Tamas, indifference. In Section V a creation myth is set out, according to which the highest produces the three Guṇas, Tamas, Rajas and Sattva, and from Sattva, spirit, consisting of pure intellect, possessing the powers of representation, judgment and individuation as its psychic body. In the hymn of Kutsâyana, an otherwise unknown sage, which precedes this myth, we find the identity of all in the Brahman asserted and the first occurrence in literature of the conception that release is both for the sake of spirit and of matter, an idea which in the Sāṁkhya is converted into the view that nature strives as if for her own release for the release of another, that is spirit, though elsewhere the release of spirit is denied and the real release attributed to nature, a contradiction arising from the fact that in reality there is, and can be, no pain in nature, which is unconscious, and the pain is brought into existence by the union with spirit, whence arises consciousness. In the Upaniṣad, which recognizes a prius to both nature and spirit, the release can be and is for both alike. In vi, 10 there is found expressly stated the doctrine of the distinction of spirit and the objective world: the psychic body is produced from the primeval material, and consists of the elements from the great one, that is intellect, apparently up to the gross elements, unless the reading is slightly altered* and the series brought to a close with the fine elements. It is, however, clearly the case in the classical Sāṁkhya that the subtle portions of the gross elements are included in the psychic apparatus, and this may be the case here also.

The other Upaniṣads of this period give us little for the Sāṁkhya doctrine. In the *Muṇḍaka*, however, we find (i, 1, 8, 9; ii, 1, 2, 3) a development of principles from the all-knower to food, thence to breath, thence to the mind, thence to truth, the worlds, and actions, or from the spirit to the imperishable, thence to breath, thence to mind and the organs of sense, and thence to the elements. This exposition

* Deussen, *Sechzig Upaniṣads*, p. 337, n. 2.

clearly accepts the absolute, and follows the normal triad of absolute, nature and souls, but it differs from the *Kaṭha*, which it otherwise somewhat closely resembles, by the addition of one principle, breath, in place of the great self and the intellect of that Upaniṣad. It is clear that Prāṇa, breath, plays a cosmic function.

As the Upaniṣads do not recognize the existence of spirit as individual only, but always admit the existence of a supreme spirit, the essence of the knowledge which is to save men from constant rebirth is the knowledge of the real identity of the supreme and the individual self. The derivative character of the Sāṁkhya comes into very clear prominence in its retention of the doctrine of knowledge as the means of saving grace. In the Sāṁkhya, as there is no real connection between spirit and nature, it seems wholly impossible to understand how the false conception of such a connection can arise: the spirit is in reality purely subjective, nature is purely objective, and there is no interaction which can explain the existence of ignorance or indeed of knowledge. On the other hand, in the case of the Upaniṣads, whatever degree of reality be allowed to the individual souls of the world, it is essentially the case that there is a source of ignorance: the absolute, either by self-illusion or in fact, develops from itself a world of spirits and matter, and the knowledge which brings salvation is the knowledge that, despite the seeming multiplicity, there is no real difference between the absolute and the self, at any rate in ultimate essence. Ignorance is admitted in the Sāṁkhya as a fact, but it is a fact which has no explanation whatever, and therefore its position in the system must be traced to a form of philosophy in which it had a more just claim to existence.

Another clear proof of derivative nature is the acceptance, without comment, of the doctrine of transmigration and the accompanying doctrine of pessimism. The Upaniṣads do not show the doctrine of transmigration as fully developed: rather, as might be inferred from the fact that transmigration proper is not clearly known to any Brāhmaṇa text, they show only the origin of the system. The credit of first enunciating the doctrine as a great moral truth, that of retribution according to action by rebirth, is assigned to Yājñavalkya, who lays down the principle in the *Bṛhadāraṇyaka Upaniṣad* (iii, 2, 13; iv, 4, 2-6), though even this view has been questioned.* The idea, however, worked up into an elaborate and confused whole, in which the ideas of retribution by rebirth and the older view of punishment in hell and reward in heaven are thrown together, is found definitely in a late portion of that Upaniṣad (vi, 2) and in the *Chāndogya* (v, 3-10). The doctrine is by no means necessarily accepted in all the Upaniṣads of the older type; thus it is doubtful if it appears at all in the older portion of the *Aitareya Āraṇyaka;* on the other hand, it is clearly accepted by the *Kauṣītaki* and by the *Kaṭha*, and is later a commonplace assumption. Its full development and spread must antedate the rise of Buddhism, and it may fairly be argued that the doctrine prevailed among wide circles in India in the north by 550 B.C., and probably half a century earlier. Efforts have even been made to find the doctrine in the *Ṛgveda*, but so far without real success.

The origin of the belief has been attributed to borrowing from aboriginal tribes,† it being a common view in primitive peoples that the spirits of their dead pass into other forms of life. Traces of similar views have also been seen in occasional hints in the *Ṛgveda* of the departure of the elements of the dead to their proper abodes. The real importance of the Indian doctrine, however, is the moral tinge given to it by Yājñavalkya, while its immediate precursor in the Brāhmaṇas is the dread of repeated death, which is expressed in the view that even after death death may await the man who is not proficient in some ritual performance.‡ This conception of Punarmṛtyu, repeated death, for a time evidently played a considerable place in the ideas of the Brāhmaṇas, as is seen by the quite frequent occurrence of the conception in the *Śatapatha Brāhmaṇa* and by its mention in the *Kauṣītaki Brāhmaṇa*, and the turning of a ritual

* See F. O. Schrader, *Z.D.M.G.*, lxiv, 333-335.

† A. E. Gough, *Philosophy of the Upaniṣads*, pp. 20-25.

‡ See S. Lévi, *La Doctrine du Sacrifice*, pp. 93ff.; P. Oltramare, *L'histoire des Idées Théosophiques*, i, 96 ff.

conception into a moral one was as natural as the transfer of the repetition of birth in the world beyond to the birth in this world, which was the one thing wanting to make the conception really a doctrine of transmigration. This step is not certainly taken in any passage of the *Śatapatha Brāhmaṇa*, though a few passages are open to this interpretation. In making the decisive change it is, of course, perfectly possible that the popular ideas of the spirit of the ancestor taking up its abode in some beast or bird or other form, such as that of a snake, may have helped the conception to take root and become easily appreciated. It is indeed doubtful whether without some such backgrond we could explain the extraordinary success of the doctrine in winning the real and lasting adherence of the great mass of the people of India. None the less, it must remain extraordinary that none of the philosophical systems should have attempted to examine the validity of the belief, a fact which stands in striking contrast with the procedure of Plato, who, in the *Phaedo*, provides a philosophic background for the conception, which he probably took direct from the popular Pythagorean or Orphic conception of the fate of the soul.

The pessimism which is assumed by the Sāṁkhya must likewise be derivative. In the Upaniṣads there is no general pessimism visible in the earlier expositions of doctrine; the marked pessimism of the *Maitrāyaṇī* is a clear indication of its posteriority to the influence of Buddhism, which had evidently a very considerable part in spreading the doctrine. The underlying view of the Upaniṣads is, indeed, that the Ātman in itself is perfect, and that, accordingly, all else is filled with trouble, as the *Bṛhadāraṇyaka* (iii, 4, 2; 5, 1; 7, 23) expressly says; and with this expression of opinion may be set such remarks as that the knower of the self overcomes sorrow; nor is there any lack of references to old age and trouble. But it is one thing to admit this, and quite another to hold that the general tone of the Upaniṣads is pessimistic; rather the joy of the discovery of the new knowledge is the characteristic of the teachers, while they regard the self as in itself bliss. Since the knowledge of the self is open to all, and since by that knowledge bliss is to be obtained, the older Upaniṣads could not be and are not pessimistic. While, however, the Sāṁkhya shares with them the belief in the possibility of freedom being obtained in the course of man's lifetime, and thus has a less pessimistic side, it denies that there is bliss in the state of the released spirit, and like Buddhism dwells on the reality of human misery.

Efforts have been made to find references to distinctively Sāṁkhya doctrines in older Upaniṣads, such as the *Chāndogya* and the *Bṛhadāraṇyaka.* In the latter text (iv, 4, 8) the term Liṅga appears beside mind, and the suggestion to treat it as meaning psychic apparatus* presents itself, but it is much more likely that the sense is simply "bearing a characteristic mark." In iv, 4, 13, a verse found also in *Īśā Upaniṣad* 12, Śaṁkara sees a reference to the Sāṁkhya doctrine in the term Asambhūti which he renders as Prakṛti, but this view has in itself no probability, and the commentator, Uvaṭa, declares that the polemic against the believers in Asambhūti, destruction, is directed against the materialists. The statement in i, 4, 15, of the Upaniṣad, that in the beginning the universe was undiscriminated, and was later discriminated by name and form, is a repetition of a very old concept, which has had its share in moulding the Sāṁkhya concept of Prakṛti, but it is not specifically Sāṁkhya. The *Chāndogya Upaniṣad* in vii, 25,1 has the word Ahaṁkāra, but uses it merely as a synonym for the self, Ātman, and in vii, 26, 2, the term Sattva has not yet the technical sense of one of the three constituents of nature which belongs to it in the Sāṁkhya. Nor in iii, 19 is there anything specifically Sāṁkhya: that paragraph is a legend of the origin of being from non-being, the coming into existence of an egg, the two halves of which are sky and earth, and from which the sun arises. This form of creation myth is of importance for the creation legends seen in Manu and the Purāṇas, but its relation to Sāṁkhya is merely the vague one that it contemplates a process of production, though the idea of not being as prior to being is completely contrary to the developed Sāṁkhya

* This doctrine is not clearly known to any Upaniṣad before the *Maitrāyaṇī* (vi, 10); *Kaṭha* (vi, 8) and *Śvetāśvatara* (vi, 9) may refer to it.

view, which does not regard Prakṛti, when unevolved, as not-being, because it is nothing definite. The conception of the Upaniṣad version with that of the cosmogonic hymn, *Ṛgveda*. x, 129, is obvious, but here also we have only an idea which later is in part adopted by the Sāṁkhya, that of an unformed primitive matter. More importance attaches to a passage in the *Atharvaveda* (x, 8, 43)

> The lotus flower of nine doors,
> Covered with three strands,
> What prodigy there is within it,
> That the Brahman-knowers know.

The human body with its nine orifices is clearly meant by the flower with nine doors, but the three strands present difficulties. The meaning " quality " is not proved for early Vedic literature, occurring first in the Sūtras, and the sense must therefore be assumed to be constituent or something similar, the reference being probably to the hair, skin and nails. If the reference is to be taken as to the constituents in the sense of the Guṇas of the Sāṁkhya philosophy,* it is clear that the expression is inaccurate, since the three constituents make up nature, and the passage would say that the body was covered with nature, instead of consisting of nature. An attempt† to find in the same hymn (x, 8, 39, 40) a reference to the doctrine of the ages of the world, there being periodic destruction and reproduction, cannot be regarded as proved, though in any case it would not be of any value as proof of the existence of the Sāṁkhya, since the idea is common to all the systems.

In the later Upaniṣads, such as the *Nṛsiṁhatāpanīya*, *Garbha*, *Cūlikā*, and others, clear references to Sāṁkhya doctrines occur, but the dates of these Upaniṣads are far too uncertain, and probably late, to throw any light on the question of the origin or of the doctrines of the Sāṁkhya.

* See Whitney's note with Lanman's correction. The Guṇa theory is accepted by P. Oltramare, *L'histoire des Idées Théosophiques*, i, 240, 241. Cf. below, p. 48.

† See H. Jacobi, *Göttingische Gelehrte Anzeigen*, 1895, p. 210. For the alleged mention in the *Aitareya Brāhmaṇa*, see Macdonell and Keith, *Vedic Index*, ii, 193.

II.

SĀṀKHYA AND BUDDHISM

THE essential fact of the atheism of the Sāṁkhya system in its classical form and the atheism of Buddhism naturally raises the problem whether the view is borrowed by the one system from the other. There is, of course, no *a priori* reason to deny the possibility of such borrowing; in definitely historical times there was clearly a lively interchange of views between Buddhism and the Brahmanical schools: the growth of logic was furthered by discoveries or developments now by the one side, now by the other, and there is striking similarity between the doctrine of void, which was brought into special prominence by the Buddhist Nāgārjuna, in the first or second century A.D., and its development into the Vijñānavāda of Asañga, probably in the fourth century A.D., which has suggested the view* that the illusion theory of the Vedānta, which has attained its classical shape in the doctrine of Śaṁkara, was derived from Buddhism as regards a very important part of its content. But that Buddhism is the source of the Sāṁkhya is most improbable, since the divergence of the two systems suggests that Buddhism represents a further advance in the disintegration of the earlier philosophy of the Upaniṣads. It is true that the Sāṁkhya abandons the idea of the existence of the absolute, but it is, on the other hand, careful to retain the idea of spirit and of nature; the doctrine of Buddhism, on the other hand, has in effect abandoned these two conceptions, and has left itself with only the fleeting series of mental states as a quasi reality, from which the development of the doctrine of the void is a natural enough step. It is impossible to prove, and certainly not plausible to believe, that from so developed a doctrine as that of

* See H. Jacobi, *J.A.O.S.*, xxxiii, 51-54.

Buddhism there could have grown the Sāṁkhya, which is indeed not a believer in the absolute, but as little a believer in the view that the only existing principle is the law of movement, which in essence is the view of Buddhism.

On the other hand, the question whether the Sāṁkhya is the source of Buddhism is one of peculiar difficulty, since the classical Sāṁkhya is only attested by works of a much later date than the origin of Buddhism and, even admitting that we cannot assign the doctrines which make up the philosophy of Buddhism to the Buddha himself, nevertheless there is a considerable space of time between the records of the two doctrines. There is, indeed, in the epic evidence of the existence of the Sāṁkhya at an earlier period than in the *Sāṁkhya Kārikā*, but the doctrine there cannot be definitely ascribed to the same age as the Buddhist metaphysics, such as they are. Nor can it be denied that there is the possiblity that the Sāṁkhya and Buddhism are both products of the older faith of the Upaniṣads, derived from it without the direct influence of the other, by the laying of stress on one or other of the elements which are contained in that collection of various points of view. There is certainly no difficulty in deriving Buddhism from the earlier doctrines of the Upaniṣads. The absolute which is produced as the ultimate ground of existence is clearly very far remote from knowledge, and the possibility of knowing anything of it is denied. The self which is the chief object of interest is much more immediately real, and the essential thing about the self is the fact that it suffers transmigration according to the law of action. It is not, therefore, to be wondered at if there can arise a philosophy which is largely indifferent to theoretic questions, as first enunciated by its founder, which is concerned with the essential fact of the transmigration of the actor, and which indeed goes so far as to deny the existence of any soul proper, though it substitutes for it a fairly adequate counterpart.

The only means, therefore, of proving that Buddhism is really depended on the Sāṁkhya is to find the existence in some important Buddhist doctrine of characteristics which, are very definitely connected with the Sāṁkhya and which, if not necessarily in themselves peculiarities of the Sāṁkhya school, are nevertheless treated by it in a special manner. The attempt to bring this really conclusive form of argument to bear has been made by Jacobi,* who has sought to find in the series of twelve principles, which are used in the Buddhist view to explain the causation of misery, clear traces of their derivation from the evolution series of the Sāṁkhya. The elements of the evolution series of the Sāṁkhya are not by any means peculiar to that system, but the order of evolution and the stress laid on the evolution are matters of great importance. Jacobi further strengthens his position by the argument that the reference in the epic to the two systems of Sāṁkhya and Yoga as two and eternal is a clear indication that at the time of the epic, which he sets not later than the beginning of the Christian era, the systems were of great antiquity, that the atmosphere of thought in the time of the Buddha was filled with Sāṁkhya ideas, and that the Buddha was influenced by these ideas, and strove in his own system to produce some formula of causation which would be suitable to serve as an explanation of the origin of the misery which the Sāṁkhya and his own system so strongly affirmed. He also points out that in Aśvaghoṣa's *Buddhacarita* we have an account of a meeting between the Buddha and his former teacher, Arāḍa, in which are ascribed to the latter views which resemble those of the Sāṁkhya, as modified by the belief in the personal supreme divinity of the Viśiṣṭādvaita Vedānta. The importance of this episode, if we are to credit the account in Aśvaghoṣa, would be that it would remove the most serious difficulty in the attempt to connect with the Sāṁkhya the system of Buddhism. The latter has no trace of the doctrine of the three Guṇas, or constituents, which are present in nature and all its products according to the Sāṁkhya, and therefore if it is to be derived from the Sāṁkhya it must be traced to a Sāṁkhya which did not accept the doctrine of the Guṇas. Now the account given of Arāḍa's teachings does not mention the Guṇas, and in it might perhaps be seen evidence

* *Z.D.M G.*, lii, 1-15; *Nachrichten von den Königl. Gesellschaft der Wissenschaften zu Göttingen*, 1896, pp. 43ff. For criticisms see Oldenberg, *Buddha* (3rd ed.), pp. 443ff; *Z.D.M.G.*, lii, 681-694.

of the existence of a Sāṁkhya which did not know the Guṇas.* It is clear, however, that this argument cannot safely be pressed: the historical accuracy of the views of Aśvaghoṣa is not confirmed by the information we have. Arāḍa is known to the sacred books of Buddhism, but his doctrines are never set out in any way corresponding to the picture of him in Aśvaghoṣa, and we cannot therefore say that the account in Aśvaghoṣa has any value at all, not merely for the actual teaching of Arāḍa, but for the existence at any time of a school of Sāṁkhya, which denies the existence of the Guṇas. It may be doubted if any such school of Sāṁkhya ever was known.

The causal series of Buddhism, in which the idea of cause is only an inaccurate or popular expression, applicable in its strictness to some alone of the members, traces the miseries of existence from ignorance, through the Saṁskāras, Vijñāna, name and form, the six organs of sense, contact, feeling, desire, clinging, becoming, birth, to old age and death. The series is of very curious appearance; it has variously been declared to be one of the first of the Buddha's discoveries, and to be a late conglomerate, nor in any case is it a masterwork of expression or thought. In the view of Jacobi the whole refers but to one birth and life. The last element takes us into the midst of the sorrow of existence, which is explained by birth. The first ten members serve to explain the origin of birth, and are derived in part from the Sāṁkhya and in part from the Yoga, which Buddha well knew and which had the Sāṁkhya as the basis of its philosophic system. Avidyā, ignorance, is in the Sāṁkhya and the Yoga alike the cause of the binding of the spirit. It consists in the failure to realize the external distinction of spirit and nature. In Buddhism it means the failure to realize the four great truths concerning misery. The Saṁskāras are terms of Sāṁkhya and Yoga, expressing the impressions made upon the intellect by such

* P. Oltramare (*L'historie des Idées Théosophiques* i, 243-5) holds that the Guṇa doctrine is a later accretion to the Sāṁkhya, but without adequate grounds. See also O. Strauss, *Vienna Oriental Journal*, xxvii, 257ff, who points out the affinity of Arāḍa's views to those of the epic.

activities as thinking, feeling, willing and action, from which in due course other phenomena of the life of the soul spring forth. The Buddhist conception of the Saṁskāras is a varying one, but it is sometimes clearly analogous in character. Name and form are to be considered as really equivalent to the principle of individuation, and they naturally grow out of Vijñāna, which is nothing else than the intellect of the Sāṁkhya, which has Vijñāna as one of its functions. Moreover, the derivate character of the Buddhist system shows itself very clearly in the fact that both for ignorance and for the Saṁskāras an intellect must be assumed, which it merely admits after the Saṁskāras in the form of Vijñāna. From individuation the Sāṁkhya allows, on the one hand, the organs of sense and the fine elements, from which are developed the gross elements, to arise. This is rendered plausible by the cosmic principle of individuation for each world period, but in the Buddhist series from individuation, as name and form, the senses and their objects are derived simply and without any justification as regards the derivation of the gross world from the individual. The next element in the Buddhist series, contact, is the contact of the senses and their objects which is recognized in the Sāṁkhya-Yoga: from it results the feeling of pleasure or the reverse, which is the same as the feeling of the Buddhist series. From feeling arises desire according to both theories: from desire the motive to rebirth or becoming, which in the Sāṁkhya-Yoga is termed Adṛṣṭa, or Dharmādharmau, and in the Buddhist Upādāna, clinging.

The evidence of dependence is clearly somewhat lacking in cogency, even on the theory of the causal series adopted by Jacobi, as regards certain of the points. Moreover, the series is interpreted, on the basis of the oldest Buddhist texts very differently by Oldenberg.* He lays stress on the fact that Vijñāna is conceived as coming into existence at the time of conception as a result of the Saṁskāras, or impressions, which have been formed in the mind through ignorance in a former birth. With Vijñāna come into being

* *Buddha* (5th ed.), pp. 257-295.

name and form, the latter being definitely the corporeal side of the future being, while name hints at the personality. From name and form we are led from experience of the world through the senses to the desire, which leads to clinging to life, and thence to a further rebirth, the series thus illogically including a second rebirth, which is traced to different causes, but the main idea being merely to show the connection of misery with life. An attempt to save the theory from the grave error of bringing birth twice in is made by Oltramare,* who argues that the matter is confined to an explanation of the existence of misery, based on the arguments that man is miserable because he exists through being born: he is born because he belongs to the world of becoming: he belongs to that world because he nourishes existence in himself: this he does because he has desires: he has desires because he has sensations: he has sensations because he comes into contact with the external world: this he does because he has senses, which act: the senses act because he opposes himself as individual to the nonself; this again he does because his consciousness is imbued with the idea of individuality: this again comes from former experiences, which in their turn are derived from the lack of the correct knowledge. This is a tempting suggestion, but it is open to the serious objection that it goes a good deal beyond what is recorded, and introduces in all probability too refined a psychology. Deussen† goes so far as to hold that the system is the conglomeration of two quite different elements: the last group of members from desire onwards is a formulation of the ground of the origin of misery: the group from the second to the seventh explains psychologically the growth of the eighth, desire, while the conception of ignorance is borrowed from the Vedānta and placed at the head of the series.

The only conclusion that can be drawn from the evidence is that some of the conceptions of Buddhism are very closely

* *La formule bouddhique des Douze Causes* (Geneva, 1909).

† *Allgemine Geschichte der Philosophie*, I, iii, 164-168. His view is that Vijñāna is cosmic and produces all reality. Cf. M. Walleser, *Die philosophische Grundlage des älteren Buddhismus*, pp. 49ff., but see Oldenberg, *Buddha*, p. 263 n. 1.

allied to those of the Sāṁkhya. The most important correspondence is that in the conception of the relation of ignorance and the Saṁskāras, the impressions thus left on the mind, which cause it in the view of the Sāṁkhya to attain ever new births, until at last the true knowledge is reached, and there ceases to be the possibility of rebirth, as the source being cut away no more impressions can be formed. This conception corresponds very closely with the Buddhist, and the use of the term Saṁskāras, which is not a very natural one, possibly points to direct borrowing. A second similarity of great importance is the precise correspondence of the two ideas, of the Sāṁkhya that the essential knowledge is to realize that anything empiric is not I, and of the Buddhist that it is essential to free oneself from the delusion that there is anything which is or belongs to the self. A further point of close similarity is the fact that both systems lay great stress on the conception of causality, and that they devote deep consideration to the nature of the world-process, though there is a great distinction between the Buddhist resolution of it into a series of impressions determined causally and the Sāṁkhya conception of nature. Here, too, may be mentioned the definite correspondence between the four truths of the Buddhist system and the fourfold division of the doctrine of final release in the Sāṁkhya-Yoga. The latter falls under the heads of that from which final release is to be sought, final release, the cause of that from which release is to be sought, and the means to attain release, which are compared with the medical heads of disease, health, the cause of disease, and healing. The four Buddhist truths are misery, the origin of misery, the removal of misery, and the means to its removal, which in one Buddhist text are compared with disease, its origin, its healing and the prevention of recurrence, but the similarity is not conclusive of borrowing. Yet a further striking parallelism with the Sāṁkhya is the attitude of Buddhism towards the end of endeavour. It is perfectly plain that this is not looked upon as annihilation, however clear it is that it is metaphysically nothing else: the doctrine of the Buddha is full of the savour of Nirvāṇa, and the repeated occurrence of that term in the epic suggests that the expression was borrowed from the Brahmanical speculations by the Buddhists. Similarly in the case of the Sāṁkhya, though the attainment of knowledge would really be the end of all real existence and nothingness, it is expressly recorded that this is not the aim of the seekers after the true knowledge, who on the contrary attain isolation as something in itself enduring and perfect.

These points, as well as the common possession of the rejection of the absolute, are striking, but at the same time it must be remembered that, in addition to the absence of the doctrine of the Guṇas, there is one other case of the first importance in which the Sāṁkhya is very different from, and more advanced than, Buddhism. The Sāṁkhya goes to the logical extreme, in its treatment of the difference between spirit and all else, of attributing the whole of the apparent empiric existence to the activity of nature, though that activity is only conscious by the union of nature with spirit. It therefore postulates that there is no real union of spirit and nature: and in this result it is quite logical, but, of course, at the same time it brings about its own refutation since, if there is no union, there can be no release. In the Buddhist view the release is regarded as a real one, not as something which is unreal and unconnected with the substitute for self in Buddhism. Nor has Buddhism any of the imagery by which nature is represented as a dancer performing for the benefit of spirit, or the union of spirit and nature is regarded as the union of the lame and the blind. In this and in its elaborate series of psychological conceptions, it is clear that the Sāṁkhya as we know it is far more advanced than Buddhism.

It seems best, therefore, to draw the conclusion that Buddhism did not draw its inspiration from the Sāṁkhya in the form in which it appears even in the epic, for there the doctrine of the isolation of spirit and nature and of the three Guṇas is fully and completely evolved. We have indeed no means to assert that the Sāṁkhya or its closely related Yoga may not have existed in gradually changing shapes long before it assumed its epic form, and that there may not have existed a variety of its development which directly affected the growth of Buddhism. But we have no means to reconstruct this stage of Sāṁkhya, nor can we say whether there ever was a system under that name without the Guṇas: the period from the Upaniṣads to the epic Sāṁkhya is a long one, and must have been marked by much intellectual activity, one form of which may have been a doctrine which cannot definitely be named Sāṁkhya, and from which both Sāṁkhya and Buddhism are derived. That such an atheist doctrine should have been evolved at an early date is not in the slightest degree wonderful. There is abundant evidence of the plentiful supply of heretical doctrines in India from an early date, and an atheist philosophy* can have hardly been open to more serious objection than an idealism which placed all reality in an incomprehensible absolute, and insisted that all real things were a mere illusion.†

* The Mīmāṁsā is atheistic indeed, but it as a philosophy was doubtless held to be supplemented by the Vedānta. Nevertheless, however, it shows that atheism was not wholly un-Indian. Cf. Ganganath Jha, *The Prabhākara System of Pūrva Mīmāṁsā*, pp. 85-8.

† There is, of course, abundant later evidence of the knowledge of Buddhist teachers of Sāṁkhya, as in the case of Nāgārjuna (J. H. Woods, *Yoga System of Patañjali*, p. xviii). That the Sāṁkhya system was known to the *Dīgha Nikāya* is disproved by Rhys Davids, *American Lectures on Buddhism*, pp 25ff.

III.

THE PHILOSOPHY OF THE GREAT EPIC, AND THE ORIGIN OF SĀṀKHYA

THE process by which the Bharatan epic grew into the vast text-book of ethics and philosophy as well as of statecraft and strategy must have occupied some centuries, and there is every reason to believe that the philosophical portions were by no means the first to be added. The four main sections of philosophic import are the *Sanatsujāta-parvan* of the fifth book (chapters 40-45), the *Bhagavadgītā* in the sixth book (chapters 25-42), the *Mokṣadharma* in the twelfth book (chapters 174-367), and the *Anugītā* in the fourteenth book (chapters 16-51). Of these the *Bhagavadgītā* is beyond doubt or question the oldest, a fact which is clearly attested by metre and language alike, and even its date is very doubtful. The latest attempt to estimate it is that made by Sir R. G. Bhandarkar,* who bases on the fact that the *Bhagavadgītā* does not recognize the Vyūhas of the deity, Saṁkarṣaṇa, Pradyumna and Aniruddha, an argument in favour of the *Bhagavadgītā* dating from at least the fourth century B.C. But the argument will not bear investigation, since it rests only on the view that the *Bhagavadgītā* must have accepted and mentioned that portion of the Bhāgavata doctrine, had it been in existence at the time when the *Bhagavadgītā* was finally redacted, and this assumption has not any justification. A very different result would be obtained if we were to accept the theory that the *Bhagavadgītā* shows clear traces of the influence of the Christian Gospels, but that theory rests merely on similarities of thought and

* *Vaiṣṇavism, Śaivism and Minor Religious Systems* (Strassburg, 1913), p. 11.

language which may have their source merely in the essential similarity of human thought.* Assuming that the *Bhagavadgītā* is of independent Indian origin, Garbe† has endeavoured to show that it was originally a theistic tract, with a philosophical basis in the Sāṁkhya-Yoga system, and in this form belongs to the early part of the second century B.C., while in its present form, in which it has been affected by Vedāntism, it belongs to the second century A.D. But part of his argument rested on the theory that the reputed founder of the *Yoga Sūtra*, Patañjali, was identical with the grammarian, and therefore belonged to the second century B.C., and with the disappearance of this doctrine‡ his earlier date becomes extremely improbable. We are, therefore, left to conclude that the *Bhagavadgītā* as we have it is probably not later than the second century A.D., though even for that date there is no absolutely cogent proof. In any case, it may be assumed that its material is often older, and the same considerations apply to the other philosophical portions of the *Mahābhārata*.

The philosophy presented by the epic in the form which we have it is a conglomerate of very different views, and, what is most important, of very different views repeated in immediate proximity to one another without any apparent sense of their incongruity. There is, however, one decided characteristic which holds good for the epic philosophy, and that is its theistic tinge, which constantly intrudes, and which is natural in an epic which had a far more popular appeal than had the more philosophical speculations which are here and there referred to in it. Hence we need not be surprised that the idealistic interpretation of the Upaniṣads, which seems in all empiric reality nothing but the self-illusion of the Brahman, is represented only in the feeblest degree in the epic, and that there is no passage there which can fairly be set beside the bold declaration of the *Śvetāśvatara Upaniṣad* (iv, 10) that nature is nothing but

* See Garbe, *Indien und das Christentum* (Tübingen, 1914), pp. 253-258.

† *Die Bhagavadgītā* (Leipzig, 1905), pp. 58-64.

‡ See H. Jacobi *J.A.O.S.*, xxxi, 24-29; below, pp. 56, 57.

illusion, Māyā. On the other hand, the epic has often the doctrine of the development of the whole universe as a reality from the Brahman. Thus the self is said (xii, 285, 40) to send out from itself the Guṇas, the constituents of nature, as a spider emits a web, and the same idea of the productive activity of the Brahman is found in other shapes. Characteristic of this strain of thought, and linking it closely with the Brāhmaṇa tradition, is the statement (xii, 311, 3) that from the Brahman was created the god Brahman, who sprang forth from a golden egg, and that this forms the body for all creatures.

But in addition to this view, in which we have still all derived from one principle, there arises to prominence the view that nature is other than the self, which in this aspect begins to receive frequently the designation of spirit, Puruṣa, though it is still conceived as cosmic. Thus we learn that nature creates, but under the control of spirit (xii, 314, 12), or that spirit impels to activity the creative elements, and is therefore akin to them (xii, 315, 8). The question of the unity of spirit and reality is expressly stated and denied in the *Anugītā* (xiv, 48, 6), and elsewhere (xii, 222, 15, 16) it is expressly stated that all activity rests in nature, that spirit is never active and that it is merely delusion when spirit considers itself active, and it is made clear that spirit is not one only. The distinction of spirit as inactive and nature as all-productive is recognized in the *Bhagavadgītā* (vi, 37, 19, 29), and is often emphasized, though in other places the idea is found that while creation and destruction are the work of nature, still nature is really an emanation from the spirit, into which it resolves itself from time to time (xii, 303, 31ff).

The result of the development which transfers all activity to nature and denies it to spirit is to make the latter the subject of knowledge only, that is, to make spirit a synonym for the abstraction of subject from object in conciousness, an idea which is, of course, expressed among other conceptions in the *Bṛhadāraṇyaka Upaniṣad* (ii, 4, 14; iii, 4, 2; iv, 3, 15). In the *Anugītā* (xi, 50, 8ff) the distinction of nature and of spirit as object and subject is expressed in the clearest manner, and the subject is declared to be free from any contrasts, without parts, eternal, and essentially unconnected with the three constituents which make up nature. In this passage and elsewhere the spirit is described as the Kṣetra-jña, the knower of the place, as opposed to the Kṣetra, the body, and the relation of the two is described in terms which show that all activity belongs to the empiric self, while the real spirit is a mere spectator (xii, 194). In this aspect spirit is set over against the twenty-four principles of nature as the twenty-fifth, the former being the objects of, the latter the subject of, knowledge (xii, 306, 39, 40). But the relation of these two principles is not detailed: it is a mystery which is therefore expressed in vague terms, such as the binding of spirit in nature, or again it is said in the *Anugītā* (xiv, 50, 14) that spirit uses nature as a lamp with which it enters the darkness: the two are connected like the fly and the fig leaf, the fish and water. But it is perfectly clear that final release comes through the recognition of the fundamental distinction of the spirit and nature; on this being attained all intermixture with nature ceases for spirit (xii, 307, 20).

On the other hand, beside this enumeration of twenty-five principles, which entirely declines to recognize the existence of any personal deity and recognizes a multitude of individual spirits, there stands a view which adds a twenty-sixth principle. When the spirit realizes its distinction from nature, and attains enlightenment, it, as free from the Guṇas, recognizes nature as possessing the Guṇas and unspiritual, and it becomes one with the absolute, thus attaining its own true self, free from empiric reality, unageing and immortal. In this condition, as all duality has disappeared, the spirit ceases to have knowledge, which is essentially a result of multiplicity. From this point of view also it is possible to give an answer to the insistent problem of the number of souls, and to overcome the discrepancy between the views of multiplicity and of unity. The souls so long as they are in union with nature are numerous, but as soon as they realize their distinction from nature, they fall back into the twenty-sixth principle, which is the inner self of all corporeal beings, the onlooker, free from the Guṇas, which can be seen by no one who is connected with the Guṇas/(xii, 350, 25, 26; 351, 2-4). The holders of this view represent the Yoga of the epic, as the maintainers of the twenty-five principles alone represent the Sāṁkhya school. The statement is several times made that the two schemes lead to one end and are not fundamentally different, but this claim is made only from the point of view of the Yoga, and its inaccuracy is expressly shown by the discussion in xii, 300, where the differences of the two systems are found to lie in the fact that the Sāṁkhya disowns an Īśvara, while the Yoga accepts one; and the Sāṁkhya relies on reasoning, while the Yoga relies on the direct perception of the devotee. This passage is of importance also in showing the original force of the terms Sāṁkhya and Yoga: the first must refer not merely to the enumeration of principles but to reflective reasoning, while Yoga denotes religious practices, and in special the striving after the ideal of freedom by means of the adoption of various devices to secure mental exaltation and the severance of mind from things of sense.

The tendency to obliterate the distinction of Sāṁkhya and Yoga by insisting on their common goal, and to remove the distinction between them and the more orthodox Upaniṣad doctrine by attributing to the Yoga the Brahman as the twenty-sixth principle, is a striking illustration of the tendency of the epic to see in all the philosophic doctrines merely variations of the Brahman doctrine of the Upaniṣads. From the religious side of the epic, the Sāṁkhya system is strangely taken up into the Bhāgavata faith by the equation of the four Vyūhas of the supreme spirit Vishṇu to four of the principles of the Sāṁkhya philosophy. Thus Vāsudeva is equated to spirit, Saṁkarṣaṇa to the individual soul, Pradyumna to mind, and Aniruddha to individuation. The last three emanate each from his predecessor, and from Aniruddha comes Brahman, and from him the created world. The wise reach the unity with the highest by the way of return through Aniruddha, Pradyumna and Saṁkarṣaṇa to Vāsudeva, and it is expressly stated that the Sāṁkhyas as well as the Bhāgavatas hold this belief. In the *Bhagavadgītā* itself the unity of Sāṁkhya and Yoga is insisted upon, and the Sāṁkhya doctrine is, at least in the poem as it now stands,* overlaid by the twofold doctrine that both spirit and nature are ultimately derived from the one and the same source, which, from the point of view of the Vedānta, is the Brahman, but from the religious point of view is Kṛṣṇa.

In addition to the exposition of the fundamental principle of the Sāṁkhya, the difference between the subject and the object, there is found already in the epic many of the elements which make up the classical system. Nature is repeatedly declared to consist of three constituents, Sattva, Rajas and Tamas, which are called Guṇas, a term found in the Upaniṣads not before the late *Maitrāyaṇī* (iv, 3; v, 2). In the *Anugītā* stress is laid on the fact that these three constituents are present throughout all things, though in different degree. The three Guṇas are often regarded as the fetters of the souls, since they represent nature, and one division of men given in xii, 348, presents us with the three classes of Sāttvikas in which the quality of goodness prevails, Vyāmiśras in whom the Rajas and Tamas, desire and indifference, elements are mixed with goodness, and the Vaikārikas, in whom the quality of indifference prevails throughout, and who, indeed, with a natural inconsistence from the normal doctrine, are declared to be devoid of any portion of goodness. A doctrine of the classic Sāṁkhya occurs not rarely, according to which the qualities of goodness, desire and indifference are characteristic of the worlds of the gods, of men and of beasts and plants, respectively, and the *Anugītā* (xiv, 36-38) distinguishes three classes of beings according as through goodness they advance upwards to the world of the gods, or through desire remain in the world of men, or through indifference descend to the world of beasts and plants.

From nature, in the Sāṁkhya of the epic as in the classical Sāṁkhya, are derived the various portions of the empiric world, but on this subject there prevails in the epic an abundant profusion of views. It is clear that the

* And perhaps *ab initio*, see E. W. Hopkins, *J.R.A.S.*, 1905 pp. 384-389.

reflective spirit greatly occupied itself in devising enumerations of the portions of the self: eight was a favourite number, but the elements of the eight differ. Thus in one version they are the five senses, mind, intellect and the spirit, as Kṣetrajña (xii, 248, 17), in another for the spirit, Citta, thought, is substituted, and the spirit is reckoned as a ninth element (xii, 275, 16, 18). Even such an absurdity is achieved as when a complex of fifteen is made up of spirit, nature, intellect, individuation in two forms, as Ahaṁkāra, and Abhimāna, the senses, and their objects, and the whole complex including spirit is derived from nature. In xii, 313, however, we find enumerated, as derived from nature, the five organs of perception, the five organs of action, mind, individuation, and intellect, which in its substance corresponds with the products of the classical Sāṁkhya. A nearer approach to the later doctrine is, however, to be found in the *Anugītā* (xiv, 40-42), where the order of development and not merely the results is given: from the unevolved is produced the great self, from it individuation, from it the five elements, from them, on the one hand, the qualities of sound, etc., and on the other the five vital airs, while from individuation arise the eleven organs of sense, five of perception, five of action and mind.

In the epic the three entities, intellect, individuation and mind, have all often a fully cosmic function: they are natural expressions for the activity of a personal creator, whether developed or not from the Brahman, and as we have seen are adopted in this sense by the Bhāgavatas in the series of Saṁkarṣaṇa, Pradyumma and Aniruddha, though in that series mind and Pradyumna rank above individuation and Aniruddha. The distinction, however, between intellect and individuation is a slight one, and is not normally made: rather it is assumed that intellect *per se* involves individuation, and when both terms occur it must be held that we have a result of a further process of analysis. Beside the cosmic function of these powers they figure largely in epic psychology. The principle of individuation passes for a factor in will, and at other times describes the function of attention: it is even by a false abstraction further subdivided and appears as two species, the other being Abhimâna (xii, 205, 24). The other terms are variously explained, but it is a common idea that data are given by sense, that the mind ponders upon them or raises doubts, and that the intellect decides (xii, 275, 17; 285, 17), while the spirit is a mere spectator, a view which corresponds with the doctrine that spirit is the subject without which all these psychic processes would be blind and unconscious. On the other hand, stress is often (xii, 311; xiv, 22) laid on the fact that the senses require the operation of mind to produce perceptions: without mind there is no result, but equally without the senses mind is empty. It accords well with this view that to mind is attributed the function of dreams. Mind also, in xii, 313, is brought directly into connection with the organs of action, to which it must be conceived as conveying the commands arising from the decisions of intellect, but in xii, 299, 20 the function of acting towards the organs of action as the mind acts to the organs of perception is attributed to strength, Bala, a conception which, however, is not maintained.

The intellect is often, as in the *Kaṭha Upaniṣad*, compared to a charioteer, whose reins are mind and whose horses the senses. The traveller in the chariot is in the *Anugītā* (xiv, 51, 4) declared to be the Bhūtātman, a conception which corresponds roughly to the psychic apparatus of the classical Sāṁkhya which, consisting of mind, individuation, intellect, the ten senses, the fine elements and the subtle portions of the gross elements, accompanies the spirit in all its transmigrations. There is, however, no trace in the epic of a precisely corresponding enumeration of entities as forming part of the Bhūtātman, for the epic often does not recognize the fine elements at all.* Other terms for this migrating apparatus are Liṅga, which, however, also denotes the gross corporeal body, and Retaḥ-śarīra, seed body, which recalls the doctrine of the classical Sāṁkhya, that the gross body is producted from the seed of the subtle portions of the gross elements, which form part of the psychic apparatus.

* See O. Strauss, *Vienna Oriental Journal*, xxvii, 257-275, who, however, overstates the case.

The absence of the fine elements, Tanmātras, from the epic, results in a different position in the series of evolution for the gross elements. Occasionally these are derived directly from the absolute being, following the doctrine of the *Taittirīya Upaniṣad* (ii, 1), or from mind, but their normal source is the principle of individuation. From the gross elements spring their Viśeṣas, distinctions, the term given to the specific qualities which they possess. In the classical Sāṁkhya the introduction of the Tanmātras reduces the gross elements to an inferior position: the fine elements are without distinction, Aviśeṣa, probably because each element consists of its own nature alone, while the gross elements now themselves bear the term Viśeṣas apparently because they each contain portions of the others. This theory of the mixing of elements is found in the epic, but there is also found the very different theory by which the elements, as in the *Taittirīya Upaniṣad* arise each from the less complex, the lowest, the ether, with one quality, and the highest, earth, with five.

It is characteristic of the close affinity in many respects of the classical Sāṁkhya and the epic philosophy that the vital airs, Prāṇas, are of comparatively little importance in the latter: the former reduces them to the united working of mind and the senses, while on the other hand the Vedānta preserves them as independent elements, and attributes to them the function of preserving the vegetative life. The epic mentions them often enough, but its accounts are too confused to allow of any clear idea of their function or of the value attributed to the five varieties, Prāṇa, Apāna, Samāna, Udāna, and Vyāna. Similarly, the epic makes little of the conception Jīva, soul, which resolves itself either into the Ātman with the psychic organs of the Vedānta, or the spirit with its psychic apparatus in the Sāṁkhya.

In the ethics of the epic there prevails even greater variety of doctrine than in the more metaphysical views. The doctrine of transmigration and the theory that all action is strictly conditioned by action in a previous life is mitigated and interfered with* by the doctrine of human action

* See E. W. Hopkins, *J.R.A.S.*, 1906, pp. 581-593.

and free-will, and is further complicated by the belief in the saving power of devotion to God, and his power to help. The fate of the souls on death is described more or less closely in accord with the doctrine of the Upaniṣads: there is the way of the gods, which leads to the world of Brahman and to freedom from transmigration; there is the way of the fathers, which is the fruit of good deeds and leads back to rebirth on earth; there is the third place, rebirth as a beast or a plant, and there is also the possibility of punishment in hell. Final release can be obtained either by knowledge in the form of reflection, the Sāṁkhya way which uses the means of perception, inference and scripture, or by the practice of Yoga, which results in an intuitive perception of the final truth. The truth takes two distinct forms: in the one case the end is the recognition of the identity of the individual self and the absolute, which results in the possessor of that knowledge becoming the absolute; for in the strict sense the individual self is, as in the Vedānta, the absolute self, and not a part of it, or at least the individual is merged in the absolute, if, as often may be the case, the feeling is that the individual is for the time at least real, and release is a merger rather than an identification. This state of identification, or merger, is the state of supreme bliss, though past all comprehension and understanding, which is styled Nirvāṇa. On the other hand, there appears often in the closest connection with this view the more properly Sāṁkhya view of the goal being isolation, and the saving knowledge not that of the unity of the individual and the absolute, but the realization of the distinction between self as spirit and nature. The result of this knowledge is the freedom of the spirit from all individuality and all consciousness, the spirit being freed for ever (xiv, 47, 8ff.). This is not merely the aim of the followers of Sāṁkhya, but of the followers of Yoga also, who, despite their acceptance of an Īśvara, devotion to whom by meditation upon him is a powerful assistance to final release, nevertheless in their desire for release aim at the isolation of the souls from nature, not at union with an absolute.

Not only has the epic the terms Sāṁkhya and Yoga both in their more general sense, and also as denoting the systems with twenty-five and twenty-six principles, respectively, but the names of three teachers, who are given in the last verse of the *Sāṁkhya Kārikā* as the handers down of the system, duly appear in xii, 319, 59 as teachers of the doctrine with a twenty-fifth spiritual principle along with Jaigīṣavya, Asita Devala, Parāśara, Vārṣagaṇya, Bhṛgu, Śuka, Gautama, Ārṣṭiṣeṇa, Garga, Nārada, Pulastya, Sanatkumāra, Śukra and Kaśyapa. Of the three mentioned here and in the *Kārikā*, Kapila plays a great figure in the philosophy of the epic: he is authoritative in all philosophic matters, and his tenets are of the most diverse kinds. In the strict sense of the word he is, indeed, the only founder of a system recognized in the epic, the other persons being either gods or his disciples, He himself is identified with Agni, with Śiva and Viṣṇu: he also appears, as in the *Śvetāśvatara Upaniṣad* (v, 2), as identical with Hiraṇyagarbha (xii, 339, 68; 342, 95). Moreover, Āsuri and Pañcaśikha appear also in xii, 218, 14, as teachers of the doctrine of the Brahman. The system of Pañcaśikha* is developed in great detail in xii, 219: not only has it in detail no special connection with the Sāṁkhya, but in its fundamental principles it is not Sāṁkhya at all; on the contrary, while the separate existence for the time being of the individual soul is asserted, it is expressly made clear that it flows as a stream to the ocean, and that at the end it is merged in the great ocean of being and embraced on all sides, losing then consciousness. As the deer leaves its old horn, or the snake its worn-out skin, or the bird the falling tree, so the freed soul abandons its woe, and goes on the perfect way, leaving behind pleasure and pain without even a subtle body. In addition to this exposition of the doctrine of Brahman without illusion, Pañcaśikha differs in his psychology from the orthodox Sāṁkhya: he holds the belief in the existence of power as the sixth organ with the organs of action, corresponding to mind as the sixth of the organs of perception. He also holds that activity is produced by the combined result of knowledge, heat and wind: the first element produces the senses and their objects, separate existence, perception

* See E. W. Hopkins, *Great Epic of India*, pp. 149ff.

and mind; heat produces gall and other bases; wind produces the two vital breaths. Further, he discusses the question of the nature of deep sleep and the fact that the senses are not then really active. In both these respects, the importance attached to the vital airs and other physical bases, and in the stress laid on the question of the nature of deep sleep, Pañcaśikha is truly Vedāntic and not an upholder of the Sāṁkhya.

The degree of faith which can be attributed to this account of the views of Pañcaśikha can be judged from the fact that in xii, 321, 96-112 we have a different account of the views of that sage. Here there are thirty principles, with God* superadded. They are the ten senses and mind, power being ignored: intellect, Sattva, individuation, the general disposition, ignorance, the source, the manifestation, the unification of doubles such as pleasantness and unpleasantness, time, the five gross elements, being and not being, cause, seed and power. The source of all these factors is the unevolved, which is evolved by means of these principles, and as evolved is the individual. The way of life to be sought is renunciation. Yet another account of the principles is given in a version ascribed in xii, 274 to Asita Devala, but the details of this version deviate more and more from any normal schedule, the organs of knowledge being reckoned at eight.

The question arises whether we can, on the strength of these notices, attribute any serious value to the tradition preserved in the *Sāṁkhya Kārikā*. The answer as regards Kapila and Āsuri can hardly be in the affirmative, in the sense that the notice of the *Kārikā* receives any support from the epic. If there was ever a sage, Kapila, who expounded philosophy, he had disappeared into a mass of obscure tradition at an early date. Moreover, there is grave doubt to suspect his real existence at all, in view of the fact that he may owe his name merely to the use of Kapila in the *Śvetāśvatara Upaniṣad* (v, 2) as a description of Hiraṇyagarbha. The likelihood is that the name Kapila is

* See E. W. Hopkins, *Great Epic of India*, p. 152. F. O. Schrader (*Z.D.M.G.*, lxviii, 106, n. 3) suggests instead nature and spirit, but this seems an error.

merely that of a divinity which has, for whatever reason, been associated closely with the Sāṁkhya philosophy in its atheistic form, though it is essential to note that the association is not epic, in which Kapila is by no means exclusively an expounder of the Sāṁkhya, and where there prevails the vague idea that the Sāṁkhya is at bottom quite consistent with belief in the Brahman. Āsuri is a mere name, and we cannot possibly accept him as a historical philosopher without more proof. The epic asserts that he taught Pañcaśikha, whence no doubt comes the statement in the *Kārikā*.

The case of Pañcaśikha offers more difficulty, and he has often been treated as an authentic teacher: indeed, the Chinese tradition* attributes to him the work known as *Ṣaṣṭitantra*, though doubtless by an error. There has been seen a certain similarity between the doctrines attributed to Pañcaśikha in the few passages quoted from him in the commentary on the *Sāṁkhya Sūtra* and doctrines expressed in the epic. Thus his view of the infinitely small size of the soul may be compared with the same doctrine expressed in xii, 346, 13-18, and his view of the unenlightened individual with that expressed in xii, 310, but these comparisons do not carry us any further, as they do not by any means connect even the Pañcaśikha of the epic with the reputed Pañcaśikha of the school tradition. The only conclusion available is that the identity of the presumably actual teacher mentioned by the commentators and the epic Pañcaśikha is not proved, and that the latter, at least, certainly did not teach as he is represented any single doctrine, and certainly not a Sāṁkhya one. We have, therefore, two possibilities open to us: either we can assume that the name, Pañcaśikha, was that of an ancient sage, perhaps as may be indicated by Buddhist evidence cited below, originally a divine personage, to whom, as to Kapila, for reasons unknown to us, certain doctrines were ascribed, just as, for instance, Sanatkumāra, clearly a divine being, is cited as an authority in the epic, or that the late epic uses the

* Takakusu, *Bulletin d'Ecole Française d'Extrême Orient*, iv, 57 sq; Tuxen, *Yoga*, p. 14.

name of an actual teacher of high rank in the Sāṁkhya-Yoga school, but simply ascribes to him doctrines at random, indifferent to their inner consistency and still more to their consistency with the views which were actually held by the teacher in question. In the latter case the question arises whether Pañcaśikha can be dated early enough to render plausible his appearance in the epic, which was practically complete by 500 A.D. even as regards the philosophic portions, and which probably contained these sections much earlier than that.

The information which has been preserved as to the views of Pañcaśikha is fragmentary, but not unimportant, and the definiteness of some of these opinions suggests a real personality. The same impression of reality is borne out by the fact that Vācaspatimiśra, in his commentary on the *Yoga Sūtra*, regularly identifies as his views certain remarks quoted as from the teacher by Vyāsa in his commentary, and that views are expressly given as his in the *Sāṁkhya Sūtra*. He appears also, if we may trust Vyāsa and Vācaspatimiśra, to have styled Kapila the Ādividvān and to have asserted that he taught Āsuri, but he does not hint that he himself was the pupil of Āsuri, a fact which discredits the assertion of this fact in verse 70 of the *Sāṁkhya Kārikā*. From the form in which his views have been preserved for us* it would clearly seem that he wrote a work in prose Sūtras. The account of the three Guṇas attributed to him in the comment on the *Sāṁkhya Sūtra* (i, 127) is perfectly in keeping with the normal Sāṁkhya-Yoga view, and his doctrine of the reason of the eternal connection of spirit and nature quoted in the *Sūtra* (vi, 68) is the obviously correct one that it is due to lack of discrimination, a view much more thorough than the reply of the teachers generally that it was caused by works or that of Sanandana, who is elsewhere unknown, that it was caused by the internal body or psychic apparatus, since clearly the first answer merely gives a proximate cause, and the second not even a cause, but the mere form in which the connection expresses itself. Further, it is certainly in better agreement with the view of

* See *Yoga Sūtra Bhāshya*, i, 4; *Sāṁkhya Sūtra*, v, 32; vi, 68. See also Garbe, *Festgruss an R. von Roth*. pp. 75ff.

many spirits in the Sāṁkhya that each should be regarded as atomic, as is expressly* recorded in the *Yoga Sūtra* commentary (i, 36) as the view of Pañcaśikha: failing the recognition that the spirit must be considered as not in space, which is not achieved by any school of Indian philosophy, it is clear that with an infinity of spirits the doctrine of their infinite extent is difficult, and it is probable enough that in this view, which is accepted throughout the rest of the history of the Sāṁkhya, there is to be seen a trace of the influence of the Vedānta.

While this doctrine points to the early date of Pañcaśikha in the Sāṁkhya school tradition, it would be an error to place his date unduly high, for in the *Sāṁkhya Sūtra* (v, 32) he is cited as giving a definition of Vyāpti, pervasion, which rests on the basis that intellect, etc., and nature, etc., stand to one another in the relation of what is to be supported and the support. This definition shows that Pañcaśikha must have been familar with the terminology of the Nyāya school and, without postulating that he must have known the *Nyāya Darśana* as preserved to us, it indicates that he does not belong to an early period, for the Nyāya school is certainly, along with the Vaiśeṣika, the latest of the orthodox systems, being barely known even in the latest parts of the great epic. This fact harmonizes well with the fact that his style agrees most closely with that of the writer Śabarasvāmin, whose period has been fixed by Jacobi† as comparatively late, perhaps the fifth century A.D. There is no reason to place Pañcaśikha so late as this: it is most probable that he is older than Īśvarakṛṣṇa, who is not to be dated after 300 A.D. The date of the first century A.D., ascribed conjecturally to Pañcaśikha by Garbe,‡ may therefore be regarded as not excessively early: the evidence for the present hardly carries him beyond the second century A.D. This date would leave it open for his fame to become distorted and

* J. H. Woods, *Yoga System of Patañjali*, p. 74, suggests that Pañcaśikha's view was not general. but referred only to some particular stage of the self. This is doubtful.

† *J.A.O.S.*, xxxi, 24. ‡ *Sāṁkhya Philosophie*, p. 34.

for strange doctrines to be ascribed to him in the epic. It is, however, in keeping with his independent position that the epic should ascribe to him the older doctrine that the gross body was composed of all five elements, as against the theory of the *Sāṁkhya Sūtra* that it was made up of one only, the other four serving merely ancillary purposes.

In the Buddhist texts,* not only late but early, there is mention of a Gandhabba Pañcaśikha as in the vicinity of the Buddha: it would probably be unwise to see in this personage a reflection of the historic Pañcaśikha, as it would be necessary to bring down the affected texts very low, or to see in it an interpolation. The similarity of name is therefore to be regarded as accidental, for it is most improbable that the man should derive his name from the demon.

Another teacher of Yoga who is mentioned in the epic is Jaigīṣavya, who, according to the *Kūrma Purāṇa*, was a fellow pupil of Pañcaśikha. The one certain piece of information regarding him contained in the commentary on the *Yoga Sūtra* (ii, 54) shows him as a teacher of Yoga doctrine. His reality is, therefore, assured in a very different degree than that of Sana, Sanaka, Sanātana, Sanatkumāra, and Sanatsujāta, who with Voḍhu are given as teachers in the epic. Of these the last only, in whose name a degraded form of Buddha has been seen,† but wholly without ground, appears to have any historical reality: the list of Sāṁkhya teachers to whom an oblation of water is daily offered by the orthodox Brāhman includes his name after Kapila and Āsuri and before Pañcaśikha, while an atharva Pariśiṣṭa places him even before Āsuri. It would be unwise to place any faith on these evidences of chronology, but it is worth noting that the Chinese translation of the commentary on the *Sāṁkhya Kārikā*‡ suggests a series of teachers in which after Pañcaśikha come Garga, and Ulūka, or perhaps Voḍhu, before Varṣa and Īśvarakṛṣṇa.

In the law book of Manu, which is contemporaneous with the main body of the didactic epic, we find the Sāṁkhya

* H. Oldenberg, *Buddha*, p. 111.

† Weber, cited by Garbe, op. cit. p. 35.

‡ *Bulletin d'Ecole Française d'Extrême Orient*, iv, 59.

doctrine never mentioned by name, but in a number of points there are clear coincidences with the classical Sāṁkhya. Thus the number of forms of proof allowed is three (xii, 105), the three Guṇas are described elaborately (xii, 24-52) and in the first book there is a creation myth which has a tinge of Sāṁkhya views. In it, from a dark incomprehensible world, arose the absolute being Svayambhū, who created the waters, from which sprang a golden egg, in which, as the god Brahman, the creator came into being. Dwelling in the egg for a year, he came out and from its shell he fashioned the heaven and earth, the place between, and the ocean. Then he produced from himself mind, described as being and not being, then individuation, then the great self, all that is made up of the three Guṇas, and the five senses to grasp objects. From fine parts of the five senses and mind, mixed with portions of his own body, he created all other things. The account is clearly by no means definitely Sāṁkhya, nor can it be regarded as of special importance in the history of the system. The text contains many other much more Vedāntic traits, and its importance lies in the fact that it illustrates by no means badly the confused philosophical speculations of these popular texts. The same phenomenon is not rare in the Dharma Sūtras and Smṛtis: that of *Viṣṇu*, however, contains in chapter 97 a clear distinction between the spirit and the twenty-four other principles, it enumerates the three Guṇas, and some of its verses (xx, 25) show a marked similarity to Gauḍapāda's commentary on the second verse of the *Kārikā*.

The Purāṇas show also traces of the influence of doctrines similar to those of the epic. The cosmological accounts of these works contain here and there approximations to the evolutionary series of the Sāṁkhya, and they agree with it in the doctrine of the three Guṇas, but this point of view is in them associated to some extent with conceptions taken from the illusionist doctrine of the Vedānta, and far more with the doctrines of the sectarian Vaiṣṇava or Pāśupata schools. Thus in the *Viṣṇu Purāṇa*, while we find both nature and spirit described in terms appropriate to the Sāṁkhya principles, it is declared that

Viṣṇu, as supreme spirit, is one not only with spirit but with nature, and with time. The *Matsya Purāṇa* again finds that the three Guṇas in the great principle are identical with Brahman, Viṣṇu and Śiva. Naturally these and similar views* in the Purāṇas give us no information of worth as to the antiquity of the Sāṁkhya system or its primitive character.

The question inevitably arises as to the nature of the system of Sāṁkhya taught in the epic. The view adopted by Garbe† is that the Sāṁkhya of the epic is merely a popularizing and contamination of the true Sāṁkhya, which he considers is of too individual a type to have been produced except as the creation of some one mind. As he holds that this ingenious system was in vogue before the rise of the epic, or at least before the epic took its present shape, it is natural that so important a philosophy should have left its traces unmistakeably in the epic, and equally natural that the form in which it appears should be one far removed from the precision and clarity of the true system. To this argument the most serious objection is the fact that there is no real evidence that the Sāṁkhya philosophy existed as a complete whole as early as the period of the epic, say 200 B.C. to 200 A.D., the evidence of the priority of such a system to Buddhism being, as has been seen above, far from cogent. Nor again is there really any sufficient ground to hold that the Sāṁkhya system is the bold and original product of a single mind. On the contrary, the system on close examination can be seen to be a somewhat illogical reduction of principles which are expressed in the Brahman philosophy of the Upaniṣads, and in opposition to the theory of a rapid development must be set the far more probable theory of slow growth, which can be traced through the later Upaniṣads, the *Kaṭha* and the *Śvetāśvatara*, which have clear traces of the doctrine of evolution of principles in the Sāṁkhya manner. Moreover if, as is supposed, the

* Puruṣa and Prakṛti are often identified with the male and female principles: hence Sakti, and Prakṛti become identified, and in the Tantras Prakṛti and Sakti are one and the same, the creative first principle which is exalted even over the supreme deity.

† *Sāṁkhya Philosophie*, pp. 47-52.

full Sāṁkhya system was in existence before the epic, it is decidedly strange that the epic should practically ignore the doctrine of fine elements which that system has so clearly. On the other hand, the terminology applied in the *Kārikā* to these fine elements, and to the gross elements, the first being described as Viśeṣa, and the latter as Aviśeṣa, is decidedly unnatural and curious and contrasts sharply with the simple description of the gross elements and their characteristics, Viśeṣas, in the epic.

A very different theory of the epic Sāṁkhya is presented by Dahlmann.* In his view the epic is not, as is usually supposed, a heroic epic into which there has been put at various times vast masses of didactic and unepic material. From its earliest period the epic was, he holds, not different from what it now is: it was essentially a book of customary law and usage, which the epic tale illustrates. It follows from this view that the epic is held to be of great antiquity, and that in place of seeing in it a heterogeneous mass of contradictory views, we must see in it the expression of one single doctrine. This is the epic Sāṁkhya which represents the development of the unsystematic teachings of the early Upaniṣads. It is essentially a science of the Brahman, Brahmavidyā, but it is at the same time based on logic, Ānvīkṣikī, and while it never abandons traditional foundations—only once, and that on the doctrine of Ahiṁsā, which he supports against tradition, is Kapila pronounced the holder of an unorthodox view in the epic—still it freely uses the processes of reasoning. Its special aim is the investigation and setting forth of the number of principles involved and their evolution from the absolute. It is atheistic merely in the sense that it denies any personal deity such as that accepted by the Yoga, but not in the sense that it denies the absolute and impersonal Brahman, which on the contrary it unquestionably recognizes, and in which the individual soul finds Nirvāṇa. But beside the absolute it recognizes the existence of a material nature, which is the source of the manifold character of the empiric self, since

* *Nirvāṇa* (1897) and *Sāṁkhya Philosophie* (1902). Cf. A. E. Gough, *Philosophy of the Upaniṣads*, pp. 200ff; S. K. Belvarkar *Bhandarkar Commemoration Volume*, pp. 181-184.

through it the absolute becomes multiplied, and it sets itself to define in detail nature and its workings. It is merely in its substance a clearing up of the doctrines which are contained in the older Upaniṣads, such as the *Bṛhadāraṇyaka* and the *Chāndogya:* these texts lay great stress on the fact that there is one self or absolute, and that all else is not true reality, and that it is a mistake which leads to transmigration to believe that the empiric is the true reality. But these Upaniṣads do not deal distinctly with the nature of the empiric reality: the question whether it is merely an illusion is not discussed and the doctrine of mere illusion is not set out, though no doubt the extreme stress laid on the unreality of the world of experience, from the point of view of true reality, tends to render the growth of this doctrine not unnatural. Ultimately the epic Sāṁkhya with its logical theory of the Brahman becomes, on the one hand, the classical Sāṁkhya which has learned to do without the Brahman, and on the other hand, by the laying of increased stress on the unreality of the world is developed the illusion theory of Śaṁkara. Dahlmann traces the origin of the theory not merely back to the older Upaniṣads: he sees in the hymn of the *Ṛgveda*, x, 129, the creation of the universe from an indefinite substance described as water by an absolute already existing, and he considers that the fact that the Ātman is called the twenty-fifth in the *Śatapatha* and *Śāñkhāyana Brāhmaṇas* is a foreshadowing of the twenty-four principles of the Sāṁkhya other than the self, while the three Guṇas he finds adumbrated in the *Atharvaveda*, where (x, 8, 43) mention is made of the nine-doored lotus with three coverings in which there is a soul, a theory which has, as we have seen, no probability.

It is clear that the theory of Dahlmann is extremely ingenious, and it is of minor importance that the efforts to trace the twenty-fifth principle as Ātman is probably based on the mistaken rendering of Ātman as self instead of trunk of the body, as opposed to the hands, feet, fingers and toes, which are the other twenty-four principles. It is a different thing to conjecture that this fondness for the number twenty-five which is often seen in the Brāhmaṇas, where Prajāpati is described as twenty-five fold, is not one of the sources of the doctrine that there are twenty-five principles. But the attempt to hold that the epic is a unity and that it teaches a unitarian philosophy is one which offends every canon of criticism and commonsense, and the main doctrine that the atheistic Sāṁkhya is really a doctrine which accepts the Brahman, but denies the personal deity of the Yoga, is a *tour de force*. The epic, which certainly is devoted to the doctrine of the Brahman and to the reverence of great personal deities, on the other hand, certainly tends to regard the Sāṁkhya system as a sort of Brahmaism, but it is perfectly obvious from the epic that the system itself was not one of this kind at all. The truth of the matter is much better expressed by Hopkins,* who finds in the epic the traces of at least six systems, Vedic orthodoxy, Brahmaism, *i.e.*, the doctrine of the Brahman but without the illusion theory, rarely the doctrine of the Brahman with the illusion theory, the Sāṁkhya, the Yoga, and the Pāśupatas and Bhāgavatas, sectarian worshippers of Śiva and Viṣṇu respectively, who adopt in their systems a good deal of Sāṁkhya-Yoga philosophy.

The rejection of Dahlmann's theory of the existence in the epic of a Sāṁkhya which acknowledged the absolute instead of reducing all to spirits and nature, as being totally unhistorical, leaves open the question whether such a doctrine is the basis of the Sāṁkhya of the epic in the sense that that system is a development from a philosophy which recognized the absolute. The alternative to this theory is the view that the Sāṁkhya is a conception based entirely on the view of the difference between subject and object, and that this conception was formed independently of the existing Ātman-Brahman philosophy, or at least in conscious reaction from it. Stress has been laid by Garbe† on the un-Brahmanic character of the Sāṁkhya philosophy, and he has attributed it in large measure to the influence of the Kṣatriyas. The force of this argument is greatly diminished by the fact that Garbe is also inclined to attribute the

* Hopkins, *Grĕat Epic of India*, p. 81.

† *Sāṁkhya Philosophie*, pp. 3ff. So J. S. Speyer, *Die indische Theosophie*, pp. 64, 107.

Brahman doctrine in large measure to the same influence, in which case it seems impossible to treat the Sāṁkhya as markedly opposed in its basis to the Brahman doctrine. In any case, the arguments for the un-Brahmanic character of the Sāṁkhya are wholly devoid of weight. The homeland of the Sāṁkhya is placed in the east by Garbe, on the ground that Buddhism, which was in his opinion derived from the Sāṁkhya, flourished in the east, and the east was certainly less completely subjected to the influence of Brahmanism than the western middle country. The argument, however, is subject to the grave defects that the dependence on the Sāṁkhya of Buddhism is not proved, and that, if it were proved, the fact would merely show that the Sāṁkhya at the time of the rise of Buddhism was of great importance in the east: it could never show that it was first produced in the east. Nor can any weight be allowed to the argument that in Kapilavastu, the birthplace of the Buddha, we are to see the name of the town of Kapila the founder of the Sāṁkhya philosophy. That Kapilavastu really meant the town of Kapila, and is not a name drawn from the description of the place, as suggested by Oldenberg*, is very doubtful, and even if the name referred to a Kapila, that this Kapila was the Sāṁkhya sage is an idea which is not hinted at in the Brahmanical tradition, which says nothing of a town connected with and named after him.

Other arguments for the un-Brahmanic character of the Sāṁkhya adduced by Garbe are the facts that the Sāṁkhya and Yoga, Pāśupata and Pāñcarātra and the Veda are set side by side as different systems in xii, 349, 67, and that the Sāṁkhya and Yoga are mentioned (ibid. 76) as two eternal systems beside all the Vedas. This, however, merely proves that these systems differed from the Vedic tradition, not that they were opposed to that tradition or that the supporters of the views of these philosophies were un-Brahmanical. Kapila, as we have already seen, appears but once in conflict with the Vedas, when he condemns sacrifice of animals, and the text plainly supports the sage in his battle for Ahiṁsā. Moreover, the Sāṁkhya never

* *Buddha*, p. 111.

abandons the right to appeal for proof to scripture, and in fact there are numerous appeals to scripture in the later Sāṁkhya texts, while the brief *Kārikā* expressly recognizes it with perception and inference as the three modes of proof. It is true that the use of scripture made by the Sāṁkhya is a more limited one than that of the later Vedānta, but the essence of the Sāṁkhya is its rationalism, and that rationalism could not develop in Brahmanical circles is an assertion for which no proof either is or can be adduced. The extraordinarily ingenious and elaborate system of the sacrifice, as thought out by the philosophers who produced the Brāhmaṇas, is a clear proof of the interest in reasoning taken by the Brāhmans.*

While there are no arguments of any value which can be adduced for the view that the Sāṁkhya is a product of un-Brahmanical circles, there is every evidence that the system is a natural growth from the philosophy of the Upaniṣads. We have seen that the Upaniṣads, in their later period of development beginning with the *Kaṭha*, show traces of the doctrines which we find in the Sāṁkhya, such as the evolution of principles, and the drawing up of classes of principles. The Upaniṣads, however, differ essentially from the Sāṁkhya in the fact that they definitely accept either the doctrine of the absolute in its pure form, as does the *Kaṭha*, or the doctrine in a theistic form, as does the *Śvetāśvatara*. There is, in detail, in the Sāṁkhya little that cannot be found in the Upaniṣads in some place or other: not only the doctrine of the Guṇas but also that of the Tanmātras can be found there, and the work of the Sāṁkhya in large measure evidently takes the form of systematizing and developing of ideas which were not the creation of the Sāṁkhya, but which required to be put into a definite system. Indeed, in one sense, the Sāṁkhya must be treated as one of the early attempts to systematize and reduce to order the somewhat confused mass of speculation found in the Upaniṣads, the characteristic feature of the systematization being the attention paid to order and the principle of development.

* See S. Lévi, *La Doctrine du Sacrifice* (Paris, 1896).

On the other hand, there must be recognized in the Sāṁkhya the definite rejection of the absolute and the substitution for the absolute, which is the real basis of the individual souls, of a multitude of spirits. These spirits if examined are clearly nothing but abstractions of the concept of subject, and are philosophical absurdities, since in the abstract there can be but one subject and one object, neither, of course, being anything without the other. To a philosophical absurdity the system can only have arrived by a historical process, and in the number of spirits we must recognize an attempt to reproduce the number of the finite souls of experience, while in the abstract conception of the essence of spirit we have a reflex of the abstract view taken of the absolute, which is represented in the *Bṛhadāraṇyaka Upaniṣad*, and elsewhere, as the unseen seer, the unthought thinker, and so forth. On the other hand, the independent position given to nature is a distinct concession to realism: nature as objective is not dependent on spirit, though it is the object of spirit and is unconscious without spirit, and though intellect—made conscious by spirit—rises from nature, and from it other things are evolved, even so in the classical Sāṁkhya there is a tendency to regard the non-organic world as in some way in direct connection with nature. The insistence on the multitude of souls and the conceding to them of quasi-individual existence and the allowing of a certain reality to the world are characteristic features of the interpretation of the Upaniṣads as set out in the *Brahma Sūtra* of Bādarāyaṇa, and in point of fact the Upaniṣads contain clear traces of a doctrine which allows to the world of matter and to the individual souls a certain reality. The purely idealistic attitude towards the absolute, which is doubtless the real interpretation of the doctrine of Yājñavalkya in the *Bṛhadāraṇyaka Upaniṣad*, is not so frequently found in the Upaniṣads as the pantheistic, while side by side with these higher forms of doctrine we often find the conception of the absolute producing matter, into which it enters in the form of the soul, from which it is but a step to the doctrine that the individual soul thus produced has some self-importance of its own and stands in a quasi-independent relation to the absolute self.

From such a position it is not very difficult to realize that the further step might be taken of holding that the absolute, which was beyond perception, was not, like nature and spirit, to be grasped by inference, and that there was no need to postulate an absolute for the explanation of the world. The step taken was a bold and decisive one, and it is on the taking of this step that the existence of the specifically Sāṁkhya system depends, but it was a step which followed naturally from the development of the philosophy of the absolute: the end of a doctrine which placed infinity in the absolute was to reduce its content to nothing.

It is now clear in what way we must regard the Sāṁkhya of the epic. It is not a blurred version of the classical Sāṁkhya, nor is there any reason to believe that the classical Sāṁkhya had already been excogitated by this period. On the other hand, it is not a Sāṁkhya which recognizes an absolute, and merely denies a personal creator: it is, apart from efforts made by the epic to torture it into more orthodox pantheism, a system which denies an absolute, and asserts instead a multiplicity of individual souls, but in the epic, as far as we can judge, it is still without some of the more characteristic of its minor doctrines, and has not achieved the completeness and, subject to its main conceptions, clarity of outline which mark its classical form.

IV.

SĀṀKHYA AND YOGA

THE Yoga philosophy, according to the epic, is a system which is ancient like the Sāṁkhya, and this parallel position belongs to the Yoga in the whole of its historical existence. The practises of Yoga, as they are revealed to us in the *Yoga Sūtra* of Patañjali, the oldest text-book of the school, contain much that is in itself a relic of very primitive conceptions of the value of psychic states of profound excitement. This tendency to attribute importance to the obtaining of such states is widespread: there is a striking example for this form of belief in the history of Greek religion in the seventh and sixth centuries B.C., and in the *Ṛgveda* itself (x, 136) there is a mention of the mad Muni, probably a predecessor of the later Yogin. It is unnecessary, therefore, to see in the Yoga practice any borrowing* from the aboriginal tribes, though we need not doubt that these tribes practised similar rites and that their influence may have tended to maintain and develop Yoga to the extraordinary popularity which it has achieved in India.

On the other hand, it is perfectly clear that the introduction of Yoga into the practice of high philosophy was natural and proper in the case of a philosophy, which, like the Ātman doctrine, denied the possibility of knowledge of the self as subject. As the *Kena Upaniṣad* (ii) has it, the self cannot be known by him who has knowledge, but only by him who has no knowledge. Hence comes the effort to subdue all the activity of senses and of mind, to empty the intellect and thus to make it ready for a new apprehen-

* Suggested by A. E. Gough, *Philosophy of the Upaniṣads*, pp. 18, 19; Garbe, *Sāṁkhya Philosophie*, pp. 185, 186.

sion, the normal aim of the mystic of all lands and places. It is to this theoretic aim that Deussen* ascribes the origin of the practice, but it is clear that in adopting the Yoga practices for this purpose the holders of the Ātman faith were not innovators, but were turning existing material to a more refined and speculative use.

The development of the Yoga theory is first clearly revealed in the same Upaniṣads as deal with those doctrines which later are adopted as part of the Sāṁkhya system that is, of the older Upaniṣads, the *Kaṭha* and *Śvetāśvatara*,, and later by far the *Maitrāyaṇī*. In the conception of Yoga, literally yoking, there seems to be an almost necessary,† or at least normal, reference to a fixing of the mind on God. The use of Yoga is, however, as well adapted to the case of the believer in the absolute Brahman as to the devotee of an individual deity: the former stage is presented in the *Kaṭha* and *Maitrāyaṇī*, the latter in the *Śvetāśvatara Upaniṣad*. The term in its technical sense also occurs in these Upaniṣads, and when opposed to Sāṁkhya it denotes doubtless the practical side of religious concentration as opposed to the theoretical investigation. It follows necessarily from this very contrast, and from the nature of the case, that Yoga could not primarily be a separate system of philosophy, and hence its natural dependence on other systems.

In the epic the relation of Sāṁkhya and Yoga is precisely as in the Upaniṣads: the two stand side by side as philosophy and religion, as theory and practice, and some details of the Yoga practise, as given, show how much the system had advanced in the direction in which it appears in the *Yoga Sūtra*. But there appears a distinct tendency to ascribe to the Yoga, as opposed to the Sāṁkhya, a twenty-sixth principle, a perfectly enlightened spirit with which the individual spirit is really identical. The Sāṁkhya is resolutely without an Īśvara, but the Yoga has an Īśvara,

* *Allgemeine Geschichte der Philosophie*, I, iii, 507.

† As held by Rājendralāla Mitra, *Yoga Aphorisms*, p. xii; P. Oltramare, *L'histoire des Idées Théosophiques*, i, 308-310. Garbe denies this explanation. Tuxen (*Yoga*, p. 32) accepts Vyāsa's rendering as Samādhi; Charpentier (*Z.D.M.G.*, lxv, 47) takes it as Praxis.

who is identified with Brahman, who is here a supreme spirit into which the individual spirit is resolved, having been in essence a part of the absolute spirit which multiplied itself. The end of Yoga is in accordance with this view, the vision of the one true self (vi, 30, 10, 12; xiv, 19, 17-19), but it is also represented in more accurate agreement with the Sāṁkhya in its atheistic form as an isolation of the spirit from matter (xii, 306, 16, 17; 316, 14ff). From the former point of view it is not difficult to see the development of the meaning of devotion to God, which it often has in the *Bhagavadgītā*, or the further sense in that text, especially in chapters three and five, of action without hope of reward or desire of reward.

The theory has often been held that Yoga was first atheistic, and that the theism of the classical system of the *Yoga Sūtra* and of the epic alike is due to a concession to popular feeling, nor is there any doubt whatever that in the *Sūtra* the connection of the divinity with the system is really a loose one.* But the theory that there was an earlier atheistic Yoga as a philosophical system is clearly not made probable by the evidence of the epic, which shows the Yoga as clearly distinguished from the Sāṁkhya by its twenty-sixth principle, though it ever tries to assimilate the Sāṁkhya to the Yoga, and both to the doctrine of the Brahman. It is, therefore, perfectly possible that the position of the classical Yoga is due to its close association with the Sāṁkhya, which has accentuated its real indifference to the idea of a deity, which is certainly not philosophically, though perhaps historically, essential to the conception of Yoga.

Now great importance attaches to the date of the *Yoga Sūtra* of Patañjali, in view of the fact that if it could be placed in the second century B.C., there would be attained a very definite date for the growth of the Sāṁkhya school with which in all essentials except atheism the Yoga agrees. Unfortunately, this view rests only on the theory that Patañjali is the same as the author of the *Mahābhāṣya*, whose date is now usually admitted to be the middle of the

* See P. Tuxen, *Yoga* (Copenhagen, 1911), pp. 56ff.

second century B.C. This view, however, cannot stand examination. It is clear that in his philosophic views as to the nature of substance and quality, the grammarian stands on a lower plane of development than the philosopher, and on the other hand the philosopher violates one at least of the grammarian's laws of grammar. Further, the Sūtra contains some doctrines which are probably late borrowings: thus in i, 40 the theory of atoms which belongs to the Vaiśeṣika is clearly referred to, nor less clearly in iii, 52 is the doctrine of the Buddhist Sautrāntika school that time consists of moments, Kṣaṇas, which are themselves forms of development of ever restless nature. This doctrine is found also in the Vaiśeṣika school, as it accords with the Atomic theory, but not until the *Praśastapādabhāṣya*. It is less certain if we can attribute to the *Sūtra* the doctrines of Sphoṭa, which belonged to the school of grammarians, and which is supposed by the commentator, Vyāsa, to be referred to in iii, 17, or that of the infinite size of the inner organ, which is seen by him in iv, 10, and which is supposed by Jacobi* to have been borrowed from the Vaiśeṣika school, in opposition to the view that this organ was of mean size, which is asserted by Vijñānabhikṣu to have been the view of the Sāṁkhya school, though this has been questioned.† More decisive is, perhaps, the fact that the *Yoga Sūtra* seems to attack the doctrine of the Vijñānavādins, and that therefore it is probably not older than the third century A.D., and probably is younger. The great supporters of that school, Vasubandhu and Asaṅga, lived in all probability about A.D. 300, but the school itself may, of course, have existed earlier, so that no absolutely certain result can be attained. It is, however, not at all unlikely that the production of the *Yoga Sūtra* was more or less directly motived by the revival of the Sāṁkhya and its definite setting out in the *Sāṁkhya Kārikā* of Īśvarakṛṣṇa, who was an earlier contemporary, according to Chinese evidence, of Vasubandhu. The attack on the idealism of Vasubandhu thus found in the *Yoga Sūtra* would be extremely natural.

* *J.A.O.S.*, xxxi, 28.

† J. Charpentier, *Z.D.M.G.*, lxv, 848; Tuxen, *Yoga*, p. 101.

It may be added that no further light on the date of either Sāṁkhya or Yoga can be gained from a notice in the *Kauṭilya Arthaśāstra*,* which ranks as Ānvīkṣikī, logical sciences, the views of the Lokāyata, the Sāṁkhya and the Yoga schools. This enumeration, if it could be established that the work of Kauṭilya was really a work of the beginning of the third century B.C., would not indeed carry the question much beyond the evidence afforded by the epic, but it would afford a more secure basis for considering the value of the epic data, but unfortunately the date of the *Arthaśāstra* is very uncertain, and may be very much later than the suggested date.† It might possibly be thought that the combination of Sāṁkhya and Yoga with the certainly atheistic Lokāyata would permit the conclusion that the Yoga was at one period atheistic, but there seems no possible ground to insist on reading such an implication into the terms, while it may be observed that the Lokāyata can only be called Ānvīkṣikī by a stretch of the imagination, since its first characteristic is its resolute dogmatic refusal to acknowledge the existence of any means of proof save perception.

* See H. Jacobi, *Sitz. der K. Preuss. Akad. der Wiss.*, 1911, pp. 732-743; followed by Charpentier *Z.D.M.G.*, lxv, 844, n. 1.

† Keith, *J.R.A.S.*, 1916, pp. 130-7; Jolly, *Z.D.M.G.*, lxviii, 355-9.

V.

THE SAṢṬITANTRA

In the last verse of the *Sāṁkhya Kārikā* it is expressly stated that that compendium of the Sāṁkhya system contains the substance of the whole Ṣaṣṭitantra, omitting only the illustrative stories and the discussions of the views of other philosophies. The verse is not original, it being agreed that the text of Īśvarakṛṣṇa terminated at verse 69, but there is no reason to doubt the correctness of the version of fact given in it. It is, however, not clear that the term Ṣaṣṭitantra represents, as has been suggested by Garbe* a special work: on the contrary the context and the wording of the verse suggest that Ṣaṣṭitantra is a term for the Sāṁkhya philosophy as a system of sixty principles. This, moreover, is the sense in which the expression was taken by the *Rājavārttika* as cited by Vācaspati. According to this account the sixty referred to are the fifty Bhāvas of the Sāṁkhya system, together with a set of ten fundamental principles, stated as the reality, unity, and purposefulness of Prakṛti, its difference from spirit and its action for the sake of spirit, the plurality of spirits, their distinction from and connection with Prakṛti, the evolution of the other principles, and the inactivity of spirit, an order of topics which may have been rendered incoherent by the exigencies of the verse. The explanation is older than the *Rājavārttika*, for it is found in the Chinese version of the commentary on the *Sāṁkhya Kārikā* made by Paramārtha in the sixth century A.D. But despite its antiquity, the explanation of the number is open to the criticism that it confounds two different principles of

* *Sāṁkhya Philosophie*, pp. 58, 59. On the *Rājavārttika* See J. H. Woods, *Yoga System of Patañjali*, p. xxii.

division: the Bhāvas should be included under the Mūlikārthas. This seems to have been realized even in the tradition of the school, for Nārāyaṇatīrtha in his commentary on the *Sāṁkhya Kārikā* gives as the ten required to make up the sixty not the fundamental principles, but spirit, Prakṛti, intelligence, individuation, the three Guṇas, the Tanmātras, senses, and gross matter, an enumeration which is clearly arbitrary and unjustifiable.

Some further light on the Ṣaṣṭitantra is thrown by the mention of that system along with the system of Kapila in the *Anuyogadvāra Sūtra* of the Jains as *Kāvilam* and *Saṭṭhitantam*, which has a parallel in the mention of the same systems as *Kāvilā* and *Saṁkhājogī* in the *Aupapātika Sūtra.** The commentator, Abhayadeva, on the latter passage explains the system of Kapila as the atheistic Sāṁkhya, and the Sāṁkhya as the theistic Sāṁkhya, treating Yoga as a separate head, but the parallelism with the first passage and the fact that only one representative of Sāṁkhya-Yoga is given, show that but one system is meant, which united the two sides of Sāṁkhya and Yoga.

More light on this system is perhaps to be obtained from the *Ahirbudhnya Saṁhitā*, a text of the Pāñcarātra school, of uncertain date, but apparently with some claim to antiquity. In its twelfth Adhyāya are described the five systems, the Vedas, the Yoga, the Pāśupata, the Sātvata, and the Sāṁkhya. The latter is described as a Tantra with sixty divisions, which are set out in detail, in two series or Maṇḍalas, the first consisting of thirty-two and the second of twenty-eight. Of these the first are Prakṛtis, while the second are Vikṛtis. These terms, however, are used in a manner which differs essentially from that of the orthodox Sāṁkhya: in the first series are included all the principles of the Sāṁkhya and some other conceptions, while the second list contains the chief concepts of a practical physiology and ethics, these affections of the soul being termed Vikṛtis or modifications, because they come into existence only as a result of the activity of the creative

* See F. O. Schrader, *Z.D.M.G.*, lxviii, 101-110.

principles. The first of the principles is Brahman, the second Puruṣa, and the third Śakti, terms which point clearly to a form of the Yoga philosophy with express recognition of a God, beside spirit and matter. The following principles are fate, time, the three Guṇas, the Akṣara, probably meaning the doctrine of the imperishable character of sound, the Prāṇas, which in the Sāṁkhya are given a wholly dependent position, the Kartṛ and Svāmin Tantras, which may refer to intelligence with individuation, and mind, the five organs of perception, the five organs of action, the five fine elements and the five gross elements. The similarities of this system to the classic Sāṁkhya are not unimportant, but the differences are also great: there is in the interpretation given to Kartṛ and Svāmin no separate place whatever for the principle of individuation; the ideas of time and fate as principles are new; the place of the Prāṇas is contrary to the view of the Sāṁkhya; and the ideas of God and the Sphoṭa are not accepted by the Sāṁkhya.

Of the second series the first, the Kṛtya Kāṇḍa, appears to correspond with the doctrine of sources of action in the *Tattvasamāsa* (11). The second category, Bhoga, must refer to the fruit of works, the third, Vṛtta, perhaps alludes to the circle of becoming and passing away, the Saṁcara and Pratisaṁcara of the *Tattvasamāsa*. The fourth, the five Kleśas, are in this form specifically Yoga conceptions: the corresponding Sāṁkhya idea is the five forms of ignorance. The next head, the three forms of proof, is common to both systems. Khyāti, which follows, is an old term, denoting the distinction of spirit and being. It is followed by Vairāgya, freedom from desire, just as the two terms are mentioned in connection in the *Yoga Sūtra* (iii, 49 and 50). Then come Dharma, righteousness, and Aiśvarya, the possession of divine powers which with the preceding two categories form the characteristics of intelligence in its Sattva form, according to the classic Sāṁkhya. The next category, Guṇa, must clearly be confined to some such topic as the internal relations of the three constituents in the individual. The next head is that of the fine body, the following, Dṛṣṭi and Ānuśrāvika, presumably handled the questions alluded to in *Sāṁkhya Kārikā* 2, in which the insufficiency of empiricism and Vedic practices for the removal of misery is expounded. The categories of misery, Siddhi and Kashāya, have parallels in the Sāṁkhya in the three-fold forms of misery, the Siddhis and the Asiddhis, Viparyayas, Aśaktis and Tuṣṭis. The Samaya may have dealt with opposing views, and the last head is that of Moksha, final release.

The enumeration of topics is enough to show that there did exist some system of philosophy of the nature indicated, one which must have been closely allied with the epic Yoga system. But there is also evidence regarding the author of a work bearing the name *Ṣaṣṭitantra*, from which probably enough the term as a designation of the Sāṁkhya system may have been derived. That work is stated in a Chinese tradition* to have been composed in 60,000 Ślokas and to have been written by Pañcaśikha. The statement seems, however, to lack probability, and its origin can easily be accounted for by the fact that Pañcaśikha is mentioned as the third in the order of tradition of the doctines of the school in the *Sāṁkhya Kārikā* (70), and it is said that the doctrine was widely extended by him, words which may have been understood in the literal sense as denoting that an extensive text book was composed by him. On the other hand, there is the express testimony of the commentator Bālarāma that the author of the *Ṣaṣṭitantra* was Vārṣagaṇya, and this testimony receives some support from the fact that in his commentary on the *Yoga Sūtra* (iv, 13) Vyāsa cites a passage from the Śāstra which is expressly attributed by Vācaspatimiśra in his commentary on the *Brahma Sūtra* (ii, 1, 3) to Vārṣagaṇya, and which he seems† to have believed to be taken from the *Ṣaṣṭitantra*. This evidence, in itself far from clear, is strongly supported by the further Chinese tradition, which ascribes to Vindhyavāsa, who is in

* Takakusu, *Bulletin de l'Ecole Française d'Extrême Orient*, iv, 59.

† In his commentary on *Yoga Sūtra*, 1. c. S. K. Belvarkar (*Bhandarkar Memorial Volume*, pp. 179, 180) incorrectly ascribes to Vyāsa the mention of the *Ṣaṣṭitantra*.

all likelihood to be identified with Īśvarakṛṣṇa,* the re-writing of a work attributed to Vṛṣagaṇa or Varṣagaṇa. The term "re-writing" seems to have been actually justified, in view of the contents of the Ṣaṣṭitantra as sketched in the *Ahirbudhnya Saṁhitā*, and of the fact that the Ṣaṣṭitantra was evidently a manual of the Sāṁkhya-Yoga, and not of the Sāṁkhya in its atheistical form, and it is a reasonable conjecture that the origin of the *Sāṁkhya Kārikā* was due to an effort to set out in an authoritative form, in order to confute the doctrine of the Buddhists, a Brahmanical system which equally dispensed with the conception of God, but which avoided the difficulties attending the Buddhist denial of the reality both of an external world and of the soul.

There is nothing to contradict this hypothesis, though also nothing to establish it, in the four or five citations known of Vārṣagaṇya: † it has been suggested,‡ on the ground that one of these citations is in verse and the rest in prose, that we must distinguish two *Ṣaṣṭitantras*, of which the one sets out the doctrine of Sāṁkhya-Yoga and the other that of the Sāṁkhya, the former being composed in verse and the latter in prose. In favour of this hypothesis, however, there is no evidence of any kind available, unless it be considered that the assumption of two different texts would best explain the claim made that the *Sāṁkhya Kārikā* includes the whole meaning of the Ṣaṣṭitantra, but it is unnecessary to press this point. The claim is not made by Īśvarakṛṣṇa himself, and it was open for a later hand to hold that the essential doctrines of the Sāṁkhya were fully set out by Īśvarakṛṣṇa, even if he omitted those portions of the doctrines of the Sāṁkhya-Yoga school which were defi-

* As proved by Takakusu, l. c. Cf. Tuxen, *Yoga*, p. 14; Charpentier, *Z.D.M.G.*, lxv, 845, 846; below, p. 68.

† In the *Yoga Sūtra Bhāṣya* (iii, 53) he is cited as opposing the atomic theory of the Vaiśeṣikas; in Vācaspatimiśra's commentary on Kārikā, 47, as dealing with the fourfold character of ignorance; the Ṣaṣṭitantra citations in the *Yoga Bhāṣya*, iv, 13 and in Gauḍapāda's commentary on Kārikā 17 (and perhaps on 70) are neither specifically Sāṁkhya or Yoga. But the citation on Kārikā 17 looks like a verse fragment.

‡ Schrader, *Z.D.M.G.*, lxviii, 110.

nitely theistic. This view is confirmed by the fact that the succession of the doctrine is asserted in the first of the verses added to the text* to have been from Kapila to Āsuri and then to Pañcaśikha, for the evidence available regarding that teacher shows him, as we have seen, to have represented the Sāṁkhya-Yoga, not the atheistic Sāṁkhya school.†

* There is no real possibility of doubt that the *Kārikā* originally consisted of 70 verses, omitting 70-72 of the recorded text, and probably inserting another verse (cf. *Sanskrit Research*, I, 107-117).

† This fact invalidates the argument of S. K. Belvarkar (*Bhandarkar Commemoration Volume*, p. 181) that the *Ṣaṣṭitantra* must have arrived at a negative conclusion on the existence of God, which is in itself wholly incompatible with the contents of the text. It is also impossible to accept his views that the *Ṣaṣṭitantra* represents a stage prior to the severance of *Sāṁkha* and *Yoga*, and is prior to the *Yoga Sūtra* of Patañjali (circa 150 B.C.); a decisive proof of the incorrectness of this dating of Patañjali is given by J. H. Woods, *Yoga System of Patañjali*, pp. xv-xix.

VI.

GREEK PHILOSOPHY AND THE SĀṀKHYA

For the age of the Sāṁkhya important information might be obtained if it were possible to trace definite borrowings of Sāṁkhya ideas from the side of Greek philosophy. The 'απειρον of Anaximander has been compared with the nature of the Sāṁkhya, and the doctrines of the constant flow of things and of the innumerable destructions and renewals of the world found in Heraclitus are no doubt similar to tenets of the Indian system. Empedocles, like the Sāṁkhya, asserts the doctrine of the pre-existence of the product in the cause. Anaxagoras is a dualist, Democritus agrees with Empedocles in his doctrine of causality and believes in the purely temporary existence and mortality of the gods. Epicurus uses in support of his atheism the argument of the Sāṁkhya, that otherwise the divine nature must be accorded attributes which are inconsistent with its supposed character, and often emphasizes the doctrine of infinite possibilities of production.

Garbe* adds to these parallels, which he admits not to be conclusive evidence of borrowing, the fact that Persia was a perfectly possible place in which Greek thinkers, of whom travels are often recorded, should acquire knowledge of the Indian views, and supports his opinion that borrowing is probable by the case of Pythagoras, who is supposed to have borrowed from India his theory of transmigration, his conception of a religious community, his distinction of a fine and a gross body of the soul, his distinction of a sensitive organ, θυμός, and of the imperishable soul, φρήν,

* *Sāṁkhya Philosophie*, pp. 85-105.

his doctrine of an intermediate world between earth and sky filled by demons, the doctrine of five elements including ether, the Pythagorean problem, the irrational and other things. Into this question of the relation of Pythagoras to Greek thought and to India it is unnecessary to go, as the Sāṁkhya elements—as contrasted with the elements which are not specifically Sāṁkhya in his teachings—are negligible. Von Schroeder,* indeed, invents an older form of Sāṁkhya, which he understands as denoting reckoning, in which number played a much greater part than in the classical Sāṁkhya; Garbe thinks that Pythagoras may have invented his doctrine of number as the result of his misinterpreting the fact that the Sāṁkhya owed its name to its enumeration of principles, into the view that the Sāṁkhya made number the basis of nature. Both theories are based on a complete misunderstanding of the nature of the views of Pythagoras,† and the only possible conclusion is that we have no early Greek evidence for the existence of the Sāṁkhya school.

It is further not necessary seriously to consider the possibilities of borrowing on the part of Plato or of Aristotle, though the influence of the Sāṁkhya has been seen in the case of both. More plausible is the effort to find proof of Sāṁkhya doctrines in Gnosticism, an attempt to which there is not *a priori* any reason to take exception. The actual proofs of such influence adduced are not important: the comparison of soul or spirit to light, which does not occur in the oldest Sāṁkhya authorities, is anticipated by Aristotle, and is Platonic in essence; the contrast of spirit and matter is Platonic. Perhaps more value attaches to such minor points as the Gnostic division of men into three classes, which may be compared with the classification of men according to the predominance in them of the three Guṇas of the Sāṁkhya, and the assigning of personal existence to such functions as intellect and will. But such parallels, whatever they are worth, do not help definitely as to the date of a real Sāṁkhya.

* *Pythagoras und die Inder*, pp. 72-76.

† See Keith, *J.R.A.S.*, 1909, pp. 569-606.

On the other hand, the further effort to find Sāṁkhya influences in neo-Platonism must be held to be completely mistaken. Plotinus (209-269 A.D.) held that his object was to free men from misery through his philosophy, that spirit and matter are essentially different, that spirit is really unaffected by misery, which is truly the lot of matter; he compares the soul to light and even to a mirror in which objects are reflected; he admits that in sleep, as the soul remains awake, man can enjoy happiness; he insists on the realization of God in a condition of ecstasy brought about by profound mental concentration. Porphyry (232-304 A.D.) teaches the leadership of spirit over matter, the omnipresence of the soul when freed from matter, and the doctrine that the world has no beginning. He also forbids the slaying of animals and rejects sacrifice. Abammon, a later contemporary, mentions the wonderful powers obtained by the exercise of contemplative ecstasy. But there is nothing here that can possibly be considered as necessarily derived from India. The opposition of matter and spirit, the removal of spirit from the world of reality, and the view that the only power to approach to it is through ecstasy are the outcome of the Greek endeavour to grasp the problem brought into prominence by Plato of the contrast of spirit and matter, and the views of Plotinus are the logical, and indeed inevitable, outcome of that development.* The protest against sacrifice is as old as Greek philosophy, the winning of supernatural powers by ecstasy is a popular conception which appears in Pythagoras and beyond all others in the Bacchic religion. On the other hand, the real extent of knowledge of Indian philosophy available to Plotinus and Porphyry alike seems to have been most severely limited.

* See E. Caird, *Evolution of Theology in the Greek Philosophers* (1904), who develops in detail the deduction of Plotinus' view from Platonism. The same view is taken by P. Deussen, *Allgemeine Geschichte der Philosophie*, I, iii, 616.

VII.

THE SĀṀKHYA KĀRIKĀ

WITH the *Sāṁkhya Kārikā* we emerge from the region of conjecture and doubt, and arrive at the classic statement of the doctrine of the Sāṁkhya philosophy. It is admittedly by far the most brilliant account of the system, and its claim to be the oldest exposition of the doctrine in systematic form is challenged only by Max Müller's suggestion* that the oldest text-book of the Sāṁkhya is the *Tattvasamāsa*, a work of wholly unknown date and authorship. The claim runs counter to the title of the work, which shows it to be, like the Kārikās themselves, nothing more than a compendium of the doctrine of the school: the introduction is modern in appearance, and the technical terms which make up the greater portion of the content of the short tract are more numerous and more elaborate than anything found in the *Sāṁkhya Kārikā*. There is, therefore, the probability that the *Tattvasamāsa* represents a later period of the school than the *Kārikā*: certainty, in the absence of any source of information as to the *Tattvasamāsa*, is not to be attained.

The date of the work is approximately known. It appears to have been among the works which the Buddhist monk, Paramārtha, took with him to China in 546 A.D., and it is recorded that he made a translation of it and of a commentary on it during the last period of his literary activity, which falls in the years from 557-568, the date of his death.† This translation has fortunately been preserved, and proves the authenticity of the Sanskrit text as it now

* *Six Systems of Indian Philosophy*, pp. 318, 319; see below, p. 89.

† See Takakusu, *Bulletin de l'Ecole Française d'Extrême Orient*, iv., 1ff.

stands. Further, the Chinese tradition places Vindhyavāsa,* who must clearly have been none other than the author of the *Kārikā*, before Vasubandhu, a famous authority on Buddhist philosophy who is declared to have composed a work for the express purpose of refuting the doctrines of the *Kārikā*. There is no ground to doubt the correctness of the tradition, but the date of Vasubandhu is doubtful. It was placed by Takakusu in the last three-quarters of the fifth century A.D., from which it followed that the date of Īśvarakṛṣṇa must be fixed at about 450 A.D. But the date of Vasubandhu has been placed, on grounds of Chinese evidence which must be accorded great weight, by N. Péri† as at least a century earlier, and the period of Īśvarakṛṣṇa thus is thrown back into the fourth century A.D., where his activity finds an appropriate setting in the great revival of Indian studies under the Gupta dynasty, in the period which saw the bloom of the Kāvya and the drama.

More difficult is the question of the date of the commentary of Gauḍapāda, which has been handed down with the *Kārikā*, and which is certainly of considerable importance in determining precisely the meaning of the principles summarized in the sixty-nine Āryā stanzas of the *Kārikā*. The date of Gauḍapāda is uncertain: if he could safely be identfied with the author of the Kārikā on the *Māṇḍūkya Upaniṣad*, who seems to have been a predecessor of Śaṁkara, then he could be assigned to the first half of the eighth century A.D. But the contrast between the philosophical views of the two works is so great that identity of authorship can hardly be presumed on no better evidence than identity of name. Another date would be secured if it could be established that the commentary of Gauḍapāda was the basis of the Chinese commentary which is still preserved. But the

* S. K. Belvarker (*Bhandarkar Commemoration Volume*, pp. 175-178) argues that Vindhyavāsa really wrote a commentary on Īśvarakṛṣṇa's work, but this view is not probable. The fact that the *Māṭhara-Vṛtti* does not mention Vārṣaganya, who is an important author, cited by *Vyāsa*, tells against its accuracy rather than against the Chinese tradition.

† *Bulletin de l'Ecole Française d'Extrême Orient*, xi, 356ff. Cf. O. Franke, *J.R.A.S.*, 1914, pp. 398-401; Takakusu, ibid, p. 113.

researches of Takakusu have definitely established the fact that this commentary differs too greatly from that of Gauḍapāda to have been derived from it, and that both it and the commentary of Gauḍapāda must go back ultimately to a common source. This conclusion is incidentally confirmed by the evidence of the very full account of the *Kārikā* given by Albiruni (1030 A.D.), who actually mentions a Gauḍa as authority. His statements, however, cannot be derived entirely * from the work of Gauḍapāda, and it is clear that he used two different authorities. Who the author of this older commentary was is uncertain: there is a Chinese tradition that it was Vasubandhu himself, but this suggestion is supported by no evidence, and can easily be explained away as a misunderstanding of the fact that Vasubandhu wrote a work to refute the *Kārikā*. There is therefore plausibility in the suggestion† that the author was Īśvarakṛṣṇa himself, especially as the nature of the *Kārikā* is such as urgently to require an interpretation. If, however, this was the case, before the work was taken to China there had already been appended to it the last verses, which are not recognized by Gauḍapāda, but which are given and explained in the Chinese commentary. It is probable that Gauḍapāda's commentary was distinctly later than the original of the Chinese version: a terminus *ad quem* is given by the use of Gauḍapāda by Albiruni in the eleventh century A.D., and by his priority to Vācaspatimiśra, whose commentary on the *Kārikā* the *Sāṁkhyatattvakaumudī*, written in the ninth century A.D.,‡ ranks high among the authorities on the Sāṁkhya philosophy, and has been made the subject of several super-commentaries. Later is the commentary of Nārāyaṇatīrtha, which is of little value.

According to the *Kārikā* the end of the Sāṁkhya philosophy is to discover the means of removing the three-

* As held by Garbe, *Sāṁkhya Philosophie*, pp. 62-68.

† Takakusu, *op. cit.* p. 58. S. K. Belvarkar (*Bhandarkar Commemoration Volume*, pp. 171ff) argues that the original of the Chinese version was the *Māṭhara-Vṛtti*, which he is editing, but this cannot be proved, as derivation from a common source is still equally probable.

‡ Keith, *J.R.A.S.*, 1914, p. 1098.

fold misery of the world, that is, the commentators explain, the sorrows brought on us by ourselves, those brought by others, and those inflicted by fate. The removal of misery cannot be achieved either empirically or by devotion to religious practises. Good fortune on earth is perishable, and moreover it is not positive pleasure but freedom from misery that the wise man seeks. The practice of religion, again, is insufficient; the performance of sacrifice not only involves the slaying of victims which offends against the rule of non-injury, but the rewards of such actions are transitory, and the performer must fall back again, after the enjoyment of the fruit of his deeds in yonder world, into an earthly existence: moreover, the result of such actions leads to positive pleasure,* not to the freedom from pain which is the ideal of the sage.

The statement of the object of the system is of importance in that it brings out clearly the fundamental pre-suppositions on which the Sāṁkhya, like the other philosophical systems, rests. It is assumed as self-evident that the world is a condition of misery, that the soul is subject to transmigration, and that there is some degree of truth at least in the Vedic tradition. Whatever the origin of the doctrines in question, the first two assumptions are of universal validity for all schools of Indian thought, with the exception of atheistic and materialist Cārvākas, and the Sāṁkhya makes no effort to establish their validity. The third assumption is of much less importance from the philosophical view, for unlike the first two it has no real effect on the substance of the Sāṁkhya philosophy, but for the adherents of the system it had the great advantage of making the school rank as orthodox, and so on a higher plane not merely than the Buddhists or Jains, but even than the sectarian worshippers of Viṣṇu and Śiva.

The real mode of freedom from the misery of existence lies in the knowledge of the principles of the Sāṁkhya, the evolved, the unevolved, and the knower, but the preliminary

* So P. Deussen, *Allgemeine Geschichte der Philosophie*, I, iii, 415. The commentators hold that envy is produced by the sight of others' greater bliss.

question of the mode in which truth is to be attained is not ignored in the *Kārikā*. The three means of proof are expressly asserted to be perception, inference and correct tradition, which are sufficient, on the one hand, to establish every principle, and all of which, on the other hand, are essential to account for existence as known to us. Perception is defined to be mental apprehension of a present object, inference is declared to be threefold and distinguished by the presence of a mark and the bearer of a mark, while correct tradition is equated with the holy scripture, Śruti, rightly understood. The use of scripture, however, is restricted to those cases only which cannot be dealt with by the use of the other modes of proof, and the instances in which it has to be resorted to are reduced to such as are beyond perception by the sense and beyond inference by analogy: such cases are the Vedic gods, Mount Meru, and the Uttara Kurus, all things whose truth is vouched for in scripture, but which cannot be known by any other means. The three forms of inference are not described in the *Kārikā*, and the commentaries differ, but the commentary on the *Nyāya Sūtra* (i, 1, 5) explains them as inference from cause to effect, as from the presence of clouds to rain, from the effect to the cause, as from the swelling of the streams in the valleys to rain in the hills, and by analogy, as when we infer from the fact that a man alters his place when he moves that the stars, since they appear in different places, must move also.* In these cases in the Indian conception of logic the clouds, the swollen streams, the change of place of the stars are the mark, and the rain to come, the rain in the hills, and the movement of the stars are the bearers of the mark.

The absence of any attempt to examine more closely the nature of perception and of inference and their mutual relations is striking, and indicates how firmly fixed was the view of the system that perception gave immediate knowledge of reality, and that inference gave mediate knowledge. The,

* See Deussen, *Allgemeine Geschichte der Philosophie*, I, iii. 367-370. The third type is taken more generally as inductive by Vācaspatimiśra and Vijñānabhikṣu, see Garbe, *Sāṁkhya Philosophie*, pp. 153-154; Jacobi, *Göttingische Gelehrte Anzeigen*, 1895, p. 204. Cf. A Bürk, *Vienna Oriental Journal*, XV, 251-264.

admission by the side of these two principles, which alone were allowed by the Vaiśeṣika school, of the conception of authority, harmonises with the uncritical attitude of the school to the problem of knowledge, and with its essentially practical end, the removal of misery. The belief in the Vedic tradition from the point of view of purely scientific interest could not be accepted without examination: to the supporters of a system with a definite means of salvation the presence in the midst of their tenets of one which might not bear close examination was indifferent, since it did not vitally affect the main structure of the system.

The essentially inferior position as a means of proof, allotted to tradition, is attested by the Sāṁkhya doctrine of causality: despite the numerous passages in the sacred scriptures which might be adduced for the doctrine that non-existence was the source of being, the Sāṁkhya asserts the doctrine that the result really exists beforehand in its cause, just as the clay serves to form a pot, or the threads form a piece of cloth. For this theory five grounds are adduced: the non-existent cannot be the subject of an activity; the product is really nothing else than the material of which it is composed; the product exists before its coming into being in the shape of its material; only a definite product can be produced from each material; and only a specific material can yield a specific result. The last four arguments, which are in effect but two, rest on the perception that in the product the original material is contained, though under change of appearance, and that definite materials give definite and distinct results; the first argument, on the other hand, rests not merely on the fact that the coming into being of any object save from a definite material is not observed, but also on the argument that if a thing does not exist there can be no possibility of its doing anything. Hence it follows that in its ultimate essence causality is reduced to change of appearance in an abiding entity, a conception of great importance for the system.

From the principle of causality is deduced the fact that the ultimate basis of the empirical universe is the unevolved, Avyakta. Individual things are all limited in magnitude. and this is incompatible with the nature of the source of the universe. All individual things are analogous one to another, and therefore no one can be regarded as the final source of the other. Moreover, as they all come into being from a source, they cannot constitute that source. Further, an effect must differ from its cause, though it must consist of the cause, and therefore the empiric universe cannot itself be the final cause, but must be the product of some ultimate cause. The obvious difficulty that the unevolved cannot be perceived is met with the argument that its fine nature renders it imperceptible, just as other things, of whose existence there is no doubt, cannot be perceived; either because of their too great distance or proximity, through the intervention of a third object, through admixture with similar matter, through the presence of some more powerful sensation, or the blindness or other defect of the senses or the mind of the observer.

From the nature of the final cause follow the essential differences between the unevolved and the evolved. The products have a cause, on which they depend, and to which they are related: the source is uncaused and independent. They are many in number, and limited in space and name: the source is one, eternal and all-pervasive. They have activities, and parts: the source is immanent in all but has neither activities nor parts. They are the mark: the source is distinguished by them.

The process of development of the unevolved is through the activity of three constituents out of which it is made up, Sattva, Rajas and Tamas. The first of these constituents, or factors, is that in nature which is light, which reveals, which causes pleasure to man: the second is what is impelling and moves, what produces activity in man: the third is what is heavy and restrains, what produces the state of indifference or inactivity in man. The three constituents act essentially in close relation: they overpower and support one another, produce one another and intermingle with one another. They are compared in a homely simile to the constituents of a lamp, that is, it seems, to the flame, oil, and wick, respectively. The origin of the conception seems to be in the main psychologic, but even in the *Kārikā* it is impossible not to realize the material nature also accorded to the Guṇas. No proof of their existence is offered: it is to be inferred that they were held to be established by observation both of nature and of man.

From the possession of the three constituents, which is common to both the evolved and the unevolved, follow certain further characteristics of these entities, which form the discrimination between them and the other great principle of the Sāṁkhya, Purusha, or spirit. Unlike spirit, the evolved and the unevolved are without the power of discriminating between themselves and spirit: indeed without spirit they are wholly unconscious; they are objective only while spirit is the subject; they are common to all spirits whereas each spirit is unique; they are either creative, created or both creative and created, while spirit is neither created nor creative. While, however, it is expressly said that these distinctions arise from the possession by the unevolved of the three constituents which are likewise present in the evolved, the mode of the derivation of the characteristics is not given. Nor is this defect remedied in the account given of the arguments for the existence of the spirit as these arguments essentially assume that the nature of the unevolved and the evolved is something independently ascertained.

The arguments put forward for the existence of spirit are that the aggregate of nature must exist for the sake of something, that there must be something to be the presiding power for which the evolution of the universe takes place, that there must be a subject to experience the three constituents of the universe, that the development of the world proceeds for the sake of the emancipation of something, and that something must exist with qualities opposed to those of the universe. Further, it is deduced that there must be many spirits, since experience shows us separate birth and death, separate organs and different actions, and, further, spirit must be the reverse of nature, which is essentially one and the same to all. Similarly, by reason of the same contrast, spirit is the subject, not the object, it reaches and possesses freedom because of its power of discerning the difference between itself and nature: it is conscious, as against unconscious nature; it is without participation in activity in any form, and, unlike nature, produces nothing. Nevertheless, the empiric self is explained only by the union of spirit with nature: through this union the fine body which is a product of nature becomes, though itself without consciousness, conscious. On the other hand, though the constituents alone possess activity by reason of the uniting with spirit, spirit, really indifferent, appears as an actor. But the conjunction of the two is essentially not intended to be permanent: it is, in fact, like the union of a blind man with a lame man: spirit joins forces with nature in order that nature may be revealed to spirit, and that spirit may obtain freedom from its connection with nature.

This conception is the fundamental point of the whole Sāṁkhya system, and its difficulties are obvious. There is no possibility of mediation between the spirit which is removed from all action, and the active but unconscious nature. The famous simile of the blind man who carries on his back the lame man, and thus places his activity under the control of the directing power of the other, suffers from the fundamental difficulty that the two men with which it deals are both possessed of activity and so can co-operate. Spirit cannot act, and on the other hand nature, being unconscious, is not capable of receiving directions from the conscious spirit. Still more serious is the difficulty that, while the aim of the union of the lame and the blind is obviously the serving of a useful purpose, no such purpose can be conceived for the union of spirit and nature. Unconscious nature cannot experience misery: spirit in itself does not experience misery, and the union of the two, which results in the apparent experience of misery by spirit, which wrongly thinks that the misery which it brings to light in nature is misery which it itself endures, thus creates the very misery which it is the object of the union to abolish.

It is impossible to imagine that so complicated a system could have arisen from independent speculation on the nature of existence. The conception of spirit in the Sāṁkhya is clearly nothing more than the carrying to a further limit of the conception of the self in the teaching of the *Bṛhadāraṇyaka Upaniṣad.* The distinction of the subjective and the objective, and the recognition of the fact that the subject is in a sense opposed to the object, has led to the hypostatization of the subject as a separate entity opposed to all objectivity, and to the doctrine that the subject is somehow dragged into unsatisfactory contact with objectivity, from which is to be set free by recognizing its true nature, and its essential distinction from the object. Starting from the fact of normal consciousness the whole content of consciousness is attributed to nature, the element which makes it conscious to spirit, but, in place of the recognition of the fact that without content there can be no subject, the existence of the subject is asserted as reality, but the content of consciousness is represented as an error due to the failure of spirit to realize its true nature. While, however, the error of hypostatization of a mere aspect of the total process of consciousness is found equally in Yājñavalkya and his followers,* the Sāṁkhya makes a departure in two points of fundamental importance from the lines of the earlier philosophy. In both cases the points represent concessions to popular opinion, and in both cases, from the point of view of philosophy, the result is unsatisfactory. In the first place, in accordance with the obvious existence of many men a multitude of souls is allowed as real: in the second place, while, as in the Vedānta, much of the world is admitted to be the product of ideal elements,† a certain amount is left which remains, as will be seen, in some sense other than a product of the ideal elements.

The essential disadvantage of the introduction of these new elements into the system is that the conception of the subject cannot logically be maintained when many subjects are allowed. The epithets given to the subject in the Sāṁkhya are applicable to the abstract conception of the subject as opposed to all its content: there can be no multipli-

* *E.g.*, Max Müller's development, based in part on Kant, in *The Silesian Horseherd* (London, 1903), with F. B. Jevons's incisive criticism, *Hibbert Journal*, ii, 403-7.

† Garbe lays stress on the fact that all Prakṛti which he renders Urmaterie and its derivates are natural, not ideal. Būt this seems to go rather far: the product Buddhi and its derivates are rather unconscious mental states, philosophically a doubtful conception, but more satisfactory than the idea of their naturalism. Prakṛti, however, is more than Buddhi and is partly natural.

cation of this abstract conception as the Sāṁkhya asserts. The existence of numerous individuals who are conscious is a totally different thing, for their number and individuality are conditioned by the possession of a different objective content in consciousness, and when this is removed there would remain nothing at all, or at the most the abstract conception of subject, which could not be a multitude of individual spirits. Had the Sāṁkhya conception been that of a number of souls as opposed to spirits, no logical objection could be raised to the theory of multiplicity, but the sharp distinction of spirit and nature, and the assertion that there is no real connection between them, deprive spirit of any possible reality.

These difficulties come out in great prominence in the effort to deduce the evolution of nature for the sake of spirit. From nature arises the great one, often called intellect, Buddhi; then arises individuation, Ahaṁkāra; thence come the five organs of perception, Buddhīndriya; the five organs of action, Karmendriya, and the five fine elements, Tanmātras; from the five elements arise the five gross elements, Mahābhūtas, and from them the world. The series up to the five gross elements, including nature itself, number twenty-four, and with spirit as twenty-fifth make up the principles of the system. The first, nature, is evolvent only: the rest, save the gross elements, are evolved and evolvent, the gross elements are evolved, and spirit is neither evolvent or evolved, but this distinction is of no weight for the system. The series is in all probability of historical origin, as it finds, as we have seen, an analogue in the *Kaṭha Upaniṣad*, and perhaps for this reason its deduction is full of difficulty.

The essential conception is that from unconscious nature there is developed for the sake of spirit a whole universe, that the development takes place for each individual spirit separately, but yet at the same time in such a manner that nature and its evolutes are common to all spirits. The question, how nature, consisting of the equilibrium of the three constituents, Sattva, Rajas and Tamas, can be brought into activity at all remains unsolved: it is illustrated by the simile of the unconscious milk which flows to nourish the calf, yet nature is said to proceed for the freedom of spirit as men proceed to bring to cessation their desires. But nature is essentially other than spirit: it is not, as in the Vedānta, a production of ignorance, but is as real as spirit itself, though it is only under the influence of union with spirit that it evolves itself. But for that union the constituents, though credited with the power of action, would not alter from their condition of equilibrium.

The conception of intellect as the first evolute from nature is doubtless to be traced to the derivation from the Avyakta of the great soul in the *Kaṭha Upaniṣad* (iii, 11). This fact, and its position in the series of evolutes before the principle of individuation, suggest that the primary sense of the expression is cosmic, but the exact force of a cosmic intellect in a system which has not a creator or world-soul is difficult to appreciate, though in the Vedānta it is easy to understand how from the impersonal Brahman can be derived the personal Hiraṇyagarbha who can be regarded as the world-soul. At most the conception aimed at may be that the influence of spirit is to convert the wholly indeterminate nature into a consciousness, which for lack of principle of individuation can only be conceived as a potential consciousness. But this cosmic position of intellect is feebly grasped in the *Kārikā*, in which on the contrary stress is laid on the intellect as psychological. It is defined as the power of decision, by which it seems to be distinguished from mind, as the power which formulates the possible courses and carries out the decision, while on the intellectual side mind brings up the material for concepts which the intellect formulates.* Viewed in this light, intellect, which like all the products of nature consists of three constituents, in its Sattva aspect is distinguished by the performance of duty, knowledge, freedom from desire, and divine powers: in its aspect as Tamas it is distinguished by the reverse of these qualities, or more correctly it is the Rajas aspect which produces desire. It is clear that considered thus intellect cannot be prior to

* Cf. Deussen, *Allgemeine Geschichte der Philosophie*, I, iii, 436, 439. Garbe (*Sāṁkhya Philosophie*, pp. 252, 253) restricts mind to wish and doubt and to its connection with the organs.

mind or individuation, and that it performs a twofold and inconsistent part in the scheme.

The principle of individuation can only be understood as the principle through the action of which the several spirits become endowed each with a separate substratum, which results in the appearance of human individuals. It is impossible to interpret the principle of individuation in any real cosmic sense, as if this is done we would find ourselves faced with the conception of a really conscious world spirit, which is not accepted in the *Kārikā*. Psychologically the principle stands midway between intellect and mind: the sensations communicated through mind are referred to the self and result in a perfect concept; the suggestions of action sent up by mind are referred to the self by the action of individuation, and result in the decision of intellect, and the derivation of mind and the senses from individuation, like that of individuation from intellect, is again logically impossible.

The pyschological character of the principle of individuation is emphasized by the derivation from it in its Sattva aspect of the mind and the five organs of perception and the five organs of action, and from it in its Tamas aspect of the five fine elements, thus developing a further parallelism of the subjective and the objective elements. In each derivation the Rajas aspect plays its part, both as serving to set the other constituents in action and as actually present in the results. The five organs of perception are those of sight, hearing, smell, taste and touch; the five organs of action are the tongue, feet, hands, and the organs of evacuation and reproduction. Mind is, like these ten, an organ through which external reality is apprehended, but it has the important function of arranging the sense impressions into precepts, of suggesting alternatives, and of carying out the decisions of the will by means of the organs of action. The function of the organs of perception is merely observation, in contrast with the action of the organs of action. Mind with the organs* appears to be considered

* So Śaṁkara, and apparently Gauḍapāda. Vācaspatimiśra attributes the activity to mind, individuation and intellect.

as producing by their action the five vital airs, which in the Vedānta system are given an independent place as the supporters of the life of nutrition as opposed to the conscious life. The distinction of ten senses is not explained, save by a reference to the diverse development of the constituents.

Mind shares with intellect and individuation the peculiarity that there is no distinction between organ and function, as there is in the case of the other ten senses. In perception all four functions, the senses, mind, individuation, and intellect are active: in other cases only the latter three are employed, but their activity must rest upon the result of previous perception, a memory picture or an idea. The action in both cases may be simultaneous, or step by step, but in the former case the real sense is, it seems, that the process is too swift for the steps to be observed: thus an object is seen by the senses, the sense impression is developed into a percept by mind, related to the self by individuation, and made into a concept by intellect, or suggested decisions are formed by mind, brought into individuation, and the decision is given by intellect, whereupon mind sees to their execution. Thus in its widest sense the organ can be described as thirteen-fold: the three functions, intellect, individuation, and mind form the inner organ, the ten senses the outer organ, through which alone can the inner organ be set in activity, either directly in perception or through the influence of a former perception. The outer organ is thus bound to the present in time, the inner can deal with past and future. The organs are mutually helpful, but their ultimate aim is for the sake of spirit. The senses are the door, while the inner organ is compared to the doorkeeper. Between the organs of perception and of action there is a distinction in the nature of their objects; the former contemplate both the fine and the gross elements, including all the world under the latter head; speech has sound as its object, while the other four organs deal with all the five gross elements and the world derived from them.

The position of intellect, however, is one of special importance: all the action of the other organs is carried out for the intellect, and it works directly for spirit, producing its experience of all existence on the one hand and on the other securing the discernment of the subtle distinction between spirit and nature.

The fine elements are described as without difference in them, while the gross elements which arise from them are expressly described as possessing this quality, from which it would seem that the gross elements are considered, as in the *Chāndogya Upaniṣad* (vi, 4), where, however, there are but three elements in question, to be produced by the intermingling of the fine elements, the elements receiving their special names from the presence in them of the greater amount of the specific element, in accordance with the view of the Vedānta, in which each element consists of a half of one element and one-eighth each of the other four. The alternative view suggested by the *Taittiriya Upaniṣad* (ii, 1) under which the gross elements would arise from the compounding of the fine elements by the process of accumulation, wind, for example, having both the qualities of audibility and tactibility, is adopted by Gauḍapāda and Vācaspatimiśra, but seems to have less probability, since in it ether would have but one quality, audibility, and so could not be contrasted as a gross element with the corresponding fine element.

Together with the organs the fine elements form part of the Liñga, the psychic apparatus, which passes from life to life. The Liñga, however, includes as a necessary part of it the subtle parts of the gross elements, which serve as the seed whence the physical body springs. These subtle portions are as necessary to the psychic apparatus as the canvas to a picture or, by a less appropriate simile, a pillar to a shadow. This psychic apparatus, which is incorporeal, and is prior to the conception of time, accompanies the souls throughout transmigration, from body to body, in accordance with the rule of causality, playing like an actor various parts, a power which it possesses since it shares in the property of all pervadingness which belongs to nature. This conjunction of spirit with the psychic apparatus is the cause of misery, and lasts until the attainment of true insight.

The gross elements, however, have a further characteristic. They consist of two further portions, those described as born of father and mother, which go to make the body of the psychic apparatus, growing out of the seed in the form of the subtle portions of the gross elements, and the Prabhūtas, which form the mass of inorganic nature. These two elements grow out from the subtle portions, and thus each individual spirit is provided with a complete world of its own arising from itself. At the same time, however, it is expressly indicated that these last two portions of the gross elements fall back at death into the body of nature, and it is clear that the conception of the souls as monads is not carried out to its full extent.* The reason for the breach in the unity of the idea is obvious: it is intended to meet the case of the difficulty which arises as to the existence in the empiric world of other souls in human and other bodies, and of inorganic nature. To consider all these as developed from the fine elements separately for each spirit would seem unnatural, and though, therefore, the gross elements are expressly derived from the fine elements, and though these are derived from the principle of individuation, which cannot be cosmic, none the less these two portions of the gross elements are treated as being the same for all, not merely similar and, therefore, as cosmic. This fact reveals a realistic basis at the bottom of the Sāṁkhya conception, and suggests that nature is to some degree at least directly responsible for inorganic things, and even for the corporeal parts of organic things. Of the latter fourteen classes are enumerated, eight divine, given variously, by Gauḍapāda as Brahman, Prajāpati, Soma, Indra, Gandharvas, Yakṣas, Piśācas, and Rakṣases, five of beasts, given by the same scholiast as wild animals, domesticated animals, birds, reptiles, and plants, and one of men. In the worlds of the gods the constituent Sattva prevails, in that of men Rajas, in the rest Tamas. Of inorganic nature not a hint is given, a fact which suggests that the difficulties of its position were decidedly felt by the author.

* Cf. vv. 22, 39 and 41 of the *Kārikā:* the subtle portions seem to pick from nature the material for the *Mātāpitṛjas*. See Deussen, *Allgemeine Geschichte der Philosophie*, I, iii, 447, 448, 497; below, p 97. The objections of O. Strauss, *Vienna Oriental Journal*, xxvii, 262, are not convincing.

In its passage through the world, from body to body, in the course of time each soul, or spirit with its psychic body, is subject to determination, which cannot be deduced from its own nature as spirit nor from the psychic body, but must be derived directly from nature. This determination is afforded by the Bhāvas, psychic states, which are inseparably bound up with the psychic apparatus: the two go together so long as the spirit is not finally freed from the psychic apparatus. Each individual life starts with a definite equipment of states, and it adds others in its life: apparently those with which it starts exhaust themselves in the course of its life, and when it passes away and in due course a new life begins the new life carries with it the states accumulated in the last existence.

The direct connection of the states with nature is shown by the fact that the eight enumerated are those which have already been given as the characteristics of the Sattva and Tamas aspects of intellect. They are performance of duty and the reverse, which lead respectively to a higher place in the next life and to degradation; knowledge, which leads to final release; ignorance, which entails continued bondage; indifference to desire, which helps to loosen the bond between spirit and nature;* desire, which leads to rebirth; divine power, which leads to freedom from obstacles, and the possession of the Siddhis, perfections; and lack of divine power which has the reverse effect.

The *Kārikā*, however, gives, beside this eightfold division which is frequently referred to, another division of fifty states, divided under four heads. These are the five Viparyayas, erroneous views, the twenty-eight Aśaktis, lack of power; the nine Tushṭis, satisfactions; and the eight Siddhis, perfections. The five Viparyayas, which are comparable with the five Kleśas of the Yoga system, Avidyā, Asmitā, Rāga, Dvesha, and Abhiniveśa, are Tamas, darkness; Moha, confusion; Mahāmoha, deep confusion; Tāmisra, gloom; and Andhatāmisra, dark gloom. There are eight kinds of Tamas, explained by the commentators as the error

* See Deussen, *Allgemeine Geschichte der Philosophie*, I, iii, 451. Absorption in nature is the rendering of the commentators.

of regarding nature, intellect, individuation or the five fine elements as the soul; eight of Moha, explained as the belief of the gods that their eight perfections are not liable to be lost; ten Mahāmohas, the devotion of the gods and of men to sensations of sound, touch, colour, taste, and smell; eighteen Tāmisras, jealousy arising in connection with the ten objects of sense, and the eight Siddhis, and eighteen Andhatāmisras, the fear of losing these eighteen objects. There are eighteen Aśaktis, eleven of them the weaknesses of the ten senses and mind, and the remaining seventeen the defects of intellect which prevent the attainment of the nine Tuṣṭis and eight Siddhis. The nine Tuṣṭis consist of four internal, the belief in the winning of final release through nature, asceticism, time or good fortune, and the five outer, consisting of the renunciation of the sensations of touch, etc. The eight Siddhis, unlike the other Bhāvas, directly help to final release: they are meditation, study, scripture, the removal of sorrow caused by ourselves, by others or by fate, the winning of friends and Dāna, which would normally be deemed to refer to generosity, but which has been rendered* purification of the mind, since otherwise the Siddhis do not seem to contain anything corresponding to knowledge.

It seems hopeless to try to reconcile these two lists of states: they are too much alike to be regarded as radically different, and the obvious solution of the problem is to assume that they represent a view which was held in the school, and which developed the matter in a different way. It is, however, so strange that Īśvarakṛṣṇa should have introduced the matter without any hint of the relation of the two sets of states—except the wholly misleading one that they are the same thing—that the conjecture is justified that the verses (46-51) which deal with them are a later interpolation, added at or before the time when the last three verses were added and the statement made that the tract numbered seventy verses.

So long as the necessary knowledge of the essential distinction of spirit and nature is not attained, the spirit with

* By Vācaspatimiśra on *Kārikā* 51.

the psychic apparatus must wander from birth to birth, gathering from nature at each birth the portions of the gross elements described as born of father and mother in order to assume a physical body. All this time nature by evolving for spirit in the hope of enabling it to attain final release is like a dancer who displays herself on the stage and then retires again, her task unaccomplished. But in the end nature succeeds in her object, and like a bashful maiden seen in *déshabillé*, who withdraws for ever from the sight of the man who has seen her, nature, having fulfilled her object, withdraws from spirit for ever, when spirit has realized its essential distinction from nature. Then comes to an end the paradox by which spirit, which has really no connection with nature and is unaffected by the misery inherent in nature, considers itself bound and suffers transmigration, while nature undertakes the changes of evolution for the sake of spirit, since in herself she is not conscious of misery. In truth the spirit is not bound, does not undergo transmigration, and is not released, but these processes are applicable to nature, but only for the sake of spirit.

There is only one means by which nature can succeed in freeing spirit from fancied dependence on her, though she makes efforts in diverse ways: of the eight psychic states which are seen in intellect seven merely keep spirit fast in its bonds; with the eighth, knowledge, however, release is achieved. The knowledge which results in liberation is the realization that the spirit is not one or all of the principles, that it has no empiric existence, that nothing belongs to it, and that it does not exist as an empiric individual. The attainment of this knowledge through consideration of the facts of existence results in the cessation of the creative activity of nature: the other seven psychic states come to an end for ever, and spirit, in contentment, gazes as a mere spectator upon nature which no longer binds it. Recognizing that nature is not connected with it, spirit is indifferent to her, nature recognizing that her true character is understood ceases her activity, and, though the union of the two remains in existence even after the attainment of true knowledge, there is no possibility of further production. But as the potter's wheel continues to revolve for a time, after he ceases to maintain its motion, by reason of the acquired velocity, so the psychic states which result from the previous life have to be finally exhausted, and not until the impressions, Saṁskāras, thus existing in the mind have been removed, can the complete release be attained in death, when spirit obtains the condition of complete isolation, which is unending, and which is free from any other characteristic.

Nothing is more convincing proof of the close derivation of the Sāṁkhya from the orthodox doctrine of the Upaniṣads than the terms in which the attainment of release is described. In the system itself the doctrine of the bondage of spirit in nature is essential to explain the misery of existence, but at the same time it is admitted that there is no real bondage. No reason is given for the belief of spirit that it is bound, yet, as the bondage is unreal, it is clear that it must be produced by ignorance, since it is removed by knowledge, but this doctrine is not set out in the *Kārikā*, which on the contrary consistently treats the union of spirit and nature as a union for the final release of spirit. There is no conception of a development of spirit by its union with its opposite, resulting in a synthesis which is far more rich in content than the two factors involved: on the contrary, the connection of spirit with matter terminates with the withdrawal of spirit into a condition of absolute freedom, which must, however, at the same time be absolute nonentity. In following the doctrine of the Upaniṣads that true knowledge involves the denial of individuality, the Sāṁkhya system leads itself into the difficult position that it thus really denies the reality of its system of many spirits, since there can be no multiplicity without individuality to distinguish the several members of the group of spirits. In the Upaniṣads, on the contrary, the idea is justifiable, since the denial of individuality is due to the fact that all seeming individuals are really merely one single self. In the Upaniṣads, moreover, there is a real possibility of the binding of the self; whether the bonds be real or merely illusory, still in the first case they can be destroyed in the appropriate manner, and in the second the false belief can be removed by knowledge, but the Sāṁkhya denies any real connection whatever, and, while it therefore leaves it to be assumed that the apparent connection is caused by ignorance, it does not, like the Vedānta, elevate that ignorance into a metaphysical entity, thus leaving its existence even on the basis of the system unexplained.

In the case of any individual self, the connection of spirit and nature rests indeed on the lack of discrimination in a previous existence, which leaves its impression on the mind, and in the next existence leaves the spirit bound, but this does not meet the objection to an infinite regress which in other cases the Sāṁkhya system sharply refuses to allow. The spirit not being really connected with nature, there is no ground on which there can be produced the lack of discrimination of spirit from nature which causes bondage. In the Vedānta of Śaṁkara the finite and the infinite spirit are indeed in reality one, and the distinction between them is due to an illusion, but an illusion is something which can be removed by knowledge: a non-existing connection cannot create a lack of distinction which produces a connection. Or if that view of the Upaniṣads be accepted, in which the existence of individual souls and of the outer world is in some way believed to be real, then freedom may be won by the recognition of the true connection between the individual souls and the absolute through meditation upon, and devotion to, the absolute, or through grace, as in the *Kaṭha Upaniṣad* (ii, 23) and elsewhere.* Equally here is a connection realized between spirit and nature, the absence of which shuts off the Sāṁkhya from any possibility of logical explanation of its main principles.

* See also *Kauṣītaki Upaniṣad*, iii, 8; *Muṇḍaka*, iii, 2, 3.

VIII.

THE LATER SĀṀKHYA

SPECIAL attention has been drawn to the short tract, called the *Tattvasamāsa*, by reason of the fact that Max Müller* considered that it was the real text-book of the Sāṁkhya system anterior to the *Sāṁkhya Kārikā*. The argument in its favour is, that where it agrees with the *Kārikā* it appears to be the older: this view is not, however, supported by any detailed argument, and certainly does not seem conclusive. All that can be said of it with certainty is that Vijñānabhikṣu in his commentary on the Sūtra attributed it apparently to the same author as the Sūtra, being a brief exposition of what is said at length in the Sūtra, and that the text has, in comparatively recent times, at least in some parts of India, as at Benares, attained a popularity which is much greater than that of the *Kārikā*. The language is not marked by any special sign of date, and Max Müller thought that the different order of categories and the numerous names not elsewhere used were rather a sign of primitive and orginal character than of lateness. On the other hand, it must be said that the relegation to the end of the category of pain is certainly curious and artificial in appearance, as contrasted with the position which pain occupies at the beginning of the *Kārikā* as giving the tone to the whole system, and the fact that the term *Tattvasamāsa* shows that the work is a compendium is surely evidence against the text representing the original Sūtras of the school.

* *Six Systems of Indian Philosophy*, pp. 318ff. The later date, after 1400 A.D , is preferred by Garbe, *Sāṁkhya Philosophie*, pp. 68-70,

After an enumeration and explanation of the twenty-five principles, arranged as the eight evolvents, nature, intellect, individuation, and the five fine elements; the sixteen evolutes, arranged as the five organs of perception, the five organs of action, mind and the five gross elements; and spirit, the tract proceeds to enumerate the three Guṇas and to explain their nature. Then come brief explanations of the process of evolution and the resolution of the evolved going from nature to the material elements, and from the material elements back to nature. Thereafter the intellect, individuation, mind and the ten senses are set out as psychical and subjective over against the objects of their activity and the presiding deities, a concept which is decidedly more at home in the Vedānta than in the Sāṁkhya. Then come the five Abhibuddhis, which are forms of the activity of intellect, ascertainment, self-reference, desire, will to act and action, terms of somewhat doubtful sense and import. Then come the five Karmayonis, sources of action, enumerated as energy, faith, desire of bliss, carelessness and desire of knowledge, but also differently explained. The next topic is the five winds or vital airs, Prāṇa, expiration connected with the mouth and nose; Apāna, connected with the navel which draws downwards; Samāna, connected with the heart which moves equally about, and which has been compared, though doubtlessly erroneously, with the circulation of the blood; Udāna is connected with the throat and goes upward: Vyāna is the all-pervader. The presence of these five as a special topic is in contrast with the view of the *Kārikā*, which does not accept the vital airs as anything more than the joint working of mind and the organs. After the vital airs come the five Karmātmans, which are descriptions of the activity of the self: they are Vaikārika, the doer of good works; Taijasa, the doer of bad works; Bhūtādi, doer of hidden works; Sānumāna, the doer of what is reasonable; and Niranumāna, the doer of what is not reasonable.

The next topics discussed are the five Avidyās, the twenty-eight Aśaktis including the seventeen Atuṣṭis and Asiddhis, the nine Tuṣṭis, and the eight Siddhis. Then come the eight cardinal facts, Mūlikārthas, which are the existence, unity, purpose, and devotion to the interest of another of nature, the otherness from nature, the non-agency, and multiplicity of spirit, and the temporary union and separation of spirit and nature. The next two topics are the creation of benevolence, the production of the gross from the fine elements, and the Bhūtasarga, the divine creation in eight divisions, the animal and the vegetable creation in five, and the human creation in one. Bondage is then described as threefold, according as it is connected with belief in any of the evolvents as the highest reality, or with belief in a similar position as to the evolutes, such as is shown in devotion to objects of sense, and bondage by sacrificial gifts. This curious form of bondage arises when men through misconception give gifts to the priests, and is a distinct sign of hostility to the sacrifice, which is not seen in the *Kārikā*. Then come the three kinds of Mokṣa, release, arising from the increase of knowledge, the quieting of the senses, and lastly, as the outcome of the destruction of merit and demerit by these means, the destruction of the whole, producing the detachment of spirit from nature, and concentration of spirit upon itself. Then come three forms of proof, and finally the doctrine of misery, subdivided into three according as it is concerned with and arising from the body or mind, caused by others, or produced by fate. From this misery release can be obtained by the study of the *Tattvasamāsa*.

This summary of the contents of the *Tattvasamāsa* does not suggest that it has any special claim to antiquity: it probably represents one of several forms of arranging the Sāṁkhya principles, of which another form is preserved in the Ṣaṣṭitantra list of topics.* In any case, however, as the treatise itself is far too brief to give valuable information regarding the system, the value of the work is much inferior to that of the *Sāṁkhya Kārikā* on the one hand, or the *Sāṁkhya Sūtra* on the other.

It is probably of importance for the later date of the *Tattvasamāsa* that it is not cited by Mādhava in his account, written about 1380 A.D., of the Sāṁkhya in the *Sarvadarśanasaṁgraha*, where he uses as the basis of his exposition of the system the *Kārikā*. He also ignores the *Sāṁkhya*

* Above, Chap. V.

Sūtra itself, which thus appears to be later than his period. On the other hand, it cannot be much later, for it is commented on by Aniruddha, who wrote about 1500 A.D., and by Vijñānabhikṣu in the second half of the sixteenth century A.D. The work has also been commented on by Vedāntin Mahādeva at the end of the seventeenth century, and Nāgeśa Bhaṭṭa at the beginning of the eighteenth; the former in his comment on the last five books follows Aniruddha faithfully, in the first copies Vijñānabhikṣu, but has independent value; the latter is a mere imitation of Vijñānabhikṣu. Despite, however, the modern date, the *Sūtra* is a source of considerable importance, and may contain a good deal of old matter, though in its present form it is certainly not so pure an exposition of the system as the *Kārikā*.

This is obviously, in some measure at least, the case as regards the criticisms of other philosophies, which make up an essential part of every Indian, as of other, philosophic systems. The appended verses to the *Kārikā* expressly say that these critiques are omitted, and much of the omission may be supplied in the *Sūtra*. On the other hand, we cannot say how much : the *Sūtra* which freely uses the *Kārikā* also uses phrases borrowed from Śaṁkara, and therefore must be treated as a work the composers of which were quite capable of adding much of their own. As the text stands, practically all the leading philosophical systems receive their share of disapproval. The materialism of the Cārvākas is met by the refutation of their denial of the validity of reasoning by the reference to its self-destructive nature, since no amount of perception will give a doctrine any validity, and by the reply to the favourite argument of the production of intelligence from unintelligent things, on the analogy of intoxicating power from an aggregate of herbs, that the intoxicating power is latent in the ingredients, but there is no trace of souls in the psychic organs. The Jain doctrine of the co-extension of soul with body is refuted by the argument that, as all that is limited is temporary, souls would be temporary also. Objections are raised to the Buddhist denial of the soul, to its assertion of the momentary character of the world, and to its belief in the annihilation of personality as final release. The special doctrine of the Vijñānavādins, that nothing exists but consciousness, is refuted as well as the nihilism of the Mādhyamikas. The Nyāya and Vaiśeṣika philosophies are severely criticized: their schemes of categories are rejected as inadequate, their belief in atoms is rejected, and their denial of a primitive material is answered. The doctrine of the eternity of the mind, space, time, the ether and the atoms of the other four elements is denied, as is the atomic size of the mind, on the ground that it must have some dimension in order to act simultaneously with more than one of the senses. The derivation of the senses from the elements is equally contested. Moreover, the doctrine of causality of the Sāṁkhya, which asserts the permanence of the cause in the product is defended against the logicians' view that the product has no existence before its production and after its destruction as such. The category of inherence, Samavāya, supported by these schools is rejected in favour of the simpler view that what it means is really to be expressed by the nature of the object in question. The whole theory of soul as really active is rejected, and with it the theory that release consists in the freeing of the soul from certain characteristics. The idea of a personal deity which is accepted in the later, if not in the original form of both these philosophies, is definitely rejected, partly because it is unnecessary and interferes with the effective work of transmigration, and partly because to allow such a deity would be to leave him responsible for the misery in the world. The doctrine that the Veda is a product of a god is naturally also denied, and in its place is developed a doctrine of the recreation of the Veda at each creation of the world as a result of itself alone, in this point departing from the doctrine of the eternity of the Veda adopted by the Mīmāṁsā school, from which also the Sāṁkhya differs in rejecting the additional means of proof, such as analogy, accepted by that system, and its theories of the eternity of sound, and of the essential connection of word and sound. From the Vedānta of Śaṁkara the system differs by opposing bitterly the doctrine of the unity of soul, of the sole existence of the soul, the refusal to accept a primitive material, the doctrine of ignorance and illusion, and the view that the released soul has enjoyment as its characteristic, a view which contradicts the whole theory of the Sāṁkhya that isolation alone is the end. The Sāṁkhya also rejects, in its sister system of Yoga, the doctrine of a personal deity and of the eternity of the Sphoṭa, the concept expressed in the complex of letters of the alphabet which make up a word.* But in rejecting many of the theories of the other schools the *Sāṁkhya Sūtra* shows itself not uninfluenced by one at least of them: the work makes remarkable efforts to prove that its views are in full accord with scripture, to which it attributes conclusive value, and endeavours to show as accordant with the Sāṁkhya itself the statements in scripture regarding the personality of God, the unity in the absolute, the joy which is asserted to be part of the nature of the absolute, and the heavenly bliss acknowledged in the Vedānta as a step on the way to final release. Indeed, the text goes so far as to hold that obedience to the traditional rules of action has a good effect towards securing final release, and to talk of the attainment of the nature of the absolute.

In the main doctrines of the system the later texts throw little new or valuable light. Peculiar to them is the doctrine that the spirit throws light on the inner organ, or that the spirit serves as a mirror in which the inner organ is reflected. The importance of this doctrine lies in the fact that it is held to explain the mode in which spirit is apprehended. All perception is due to the inner organ forming in itself a picture of the thing to be perceived, which is reflected in spirit; similarly it forms such a picture of the spirit, and when the spirit reflects itself in the inner organ it brings its reflex, and therefore its self, to conscious knowledge. Another simile used to express the relation of spirit and nature which is in itself purely unconscious, is that of the reflection of the red Hibiscus shoots in a crystal near which the flower lies: the crystal remains unaffected by the reflection. Ingenious as all these comparisons are, it cannot be said that they lend

* See E. Abegg, *Festschrift E. Windisch* (Berlin, 1914), pp. 188-195.

much clearness to the subject-matter with which they deal. But they warn us of the danger of treating the evolutes of nature as being essentially material and as made into psychic states by the influence of spirit. The conception of the inner organ, consisting of intellect, individuation and mind, cannot be conceived as equivalent, as suggested by Garbe,* to the nervous system, to which psychic meaning is given by the reflection in spirit or the light thrown by spirit. Rather the conception is that everything including the psychic states of experience in an unconscious condition, is present in the inner organ, waiting to become actual by the addition of the element of consciousness given by spirit. With this view accords best the fact that the system of the *Sūtra* regards as persisting in unconsciousness in the intellect the impressions of experience which give rise to psychic dispositions, Saṁskāras.

A further development of doctrine, and not a happy one, may be seen in the treatment of intellect and individuation. The only tolerable theory is that in some way nature is converted into intellect or consciousness by the influence of spirit, and that the result of individuation is to split up this consciousness, which must be regarded as not having attained to consciousness of itself, into definite individuals possessed of definite selves. These individuals would essentially possess also individual consciousnesses, as the principle of individuation would carry with it as an essential presupposition consciousness in order to become self-conscious: this fact explains why in the *Sūtra* (iii, 9) the constituents of the inner organ, fine body or psychic apparatus, are reckoned at seventeen in place of eighteen, intellect and individuation falling under one head. From the individual principle naturally can be derived the senses with mind, and as suggested in the *Kauṣītaki Upaniṣad* (iii) the objects of the senses in the shape of the fine elements, from which the gross elements proceed, and this is clearly the main view of the *Kārikā*. On the other

* *Sāṁkhya Philosophie*, p. 255. The doctrine is probably derived from Śaṁkara's system. Cf. A. E. Gough, *Philosophy of the Upaniṣads*, p. 39.

hand, the *Sūtra* evidently regards the whole process as being a cosmic one, the principle of individuation producing cosmic organs, and elements, and the individual corresponding principles being derived from the cosmic. It is characteristic of the difficulty of the doctrine, and of its absurdity, that the explanation of the derivation is nowhere given: the Sūtra (iii, 10) merely says that from the one psychic apparatus many were produced by reason of the difference of the works, an explanation which is subject to the disadvantage that it begs the question, since the distinction of works presupposes individuals, and individuals presuppose separate psychic apparatuses with which to perform works. The probable explanation of the effort to fill up the system is to be seen in the fact that the *Kārikā* itself evidently allows inorganic nature to be in some way directly connected with nature, and not merely, as it should consistently be, derived for each individual from the fine elements which form part of his psychic apparatus.

In the third place, the *Sūtra* developes in detail the doctrine of the process of the creation and the destruction of the world, which presents in a more philosophic shape the doctrine of the ages of the world found in the epic and common to the philosophies. Nature and spirit are ever ready for creation: the former seeks to develop for the enjoyment and final release of spirit, and the latter is ready to play its part of onlooker, but, of course, it is impossible to find any beginning in time for the process. Each creation follows on a period of destruction in which everything has been resolved back into a state of inactivity, in the sense that the three Guṇas, instead of intermingling in their constant activity, merely produce each its self. Nevertheless, as soon as the result of the work done before has found the correct time, the process commences afresh, all spirits having their psychic apparatuses evolved according to the impressions left upon them by the acts done in their last existences, which have left them with a definite moral character, and with the disposition produced by their failure to recognize the separation of spirit and nature. During the period of the continuance of the world in a state of destruction, as the psychic apparatuses of the spirits are existing only in a fine condition and are not evolved, there is no difference as regards actual conditions of existence between the free and the bound spirits, but the evolution exposes the latter to all the woes of existence. In each period some escape for ever by the acquisition of the essential knowledge, but the work of nature will never be over since the total number of spirits is infinite, and the whole can thus never be released.

In the relation of the fine and the gross elements to the senses, there is clearly a difference of opinion between the *Kārikā* and the *Sūtra*. The former evidently holds the simple view that the senses can perceive the fine elements, and that it is not the gross elements alone which can thus be seen. The *Sūtra*, on the other hand, restricts to gods and Yogins the power to see the fine elements and accords to the senses the power only of seeing the gross. Moreover, it seems probable that the view of the fine elements taken in the *Sūtra* was that each of them was only the basis of the senses in question: thus sound represents the base element of sound, but not the sound which is heard, and so forth, this being the explanation of the term Aviśeṣa, without distinctions, which in the *Kārikā* points rather to the fine elements being each composed of the substance in question alone, and not like the gross elements of portions of all the others. These fine elements are expressly declared not to be indivisible, and are thus distinguished from the atoms of the Nyāya and Vaiśeṣika theory, which are rejected by the Sāṁkhya on the ground that they could never, in view of their possessing no extension, make up an extended object. Moreover, the distinction between the fine elements and the subtle portions of the gross elements, which belong, with the fine elements, to the psychical apparatus, is maintained in the later texts, in the form of the doctrine of the Ātivāhika body (iii, 12; v, 103). On the other hand, further details are given of the process of growth of the gross-body, which is really composed of earth, not of three elements, fire, water, and food, that is earth, as in the view of the Vedānta, nor of four, nor of five as in the popular view, which in the epic is attributed to Pañcaśikha himself. The other four elements aid only in producing the stability of the body: water sustains the blood, fire the heat of the body, air the breath, and ether the windpipe. The breath which in the *Kārikā* plays a very restricted part, here appears under the influence of the Vedānta as the principle controlling the growth of the body under the guidance of spirit, with which, indeed, it seems to be conceived as united even before the production of the embryo. The kind of body is determined by the power of former action, but not the building up of the body, a point in which the Sāṁkhya differs from the Nyāya and Vaiśeṣika doctrine. The other organic beings, those of station superior to man, beasts and plants are similarly composed, but plants are, though endowed with bodies, deprived according to the later texts, but not according to the epic, of outer senses, so that spirits in them cannot act, but merely undergo penance for previous actions.

The union of spirit with the inner organ, the senses, the fine elements and the body produces the empiric soul, Jīva, a term which is mainly Vedāntic, while the inner organ and the other elements, which produce from spirit the soul, are styled Upādhis, again a term proper to the Vedānta. The individual soul has, however, no real existence at all: it is not an entity; all that exists on the one hand is the body and the psychic apparatus, and on the other hand pure spirit, which is really unaffected by the Upādhis, but which by its light causes them to emerge into consciousness. Release consists in the realization that spirit is not bound by the Upādhis, and cannot be so bound. The parallelism of this view with that of the Vedānta is too marked to be accidental, and doubtless the influence of that school must here be recognized. The connection of spirit and its psychical apparatus is absolutely continuous and without beginning in time, though it can be ended: it arises from the failure to discriminate between spirit and nature, and this failure in each life is a consequence of a failure in the preceding life, which leaves in the empirical soul an impression which becomes real in its next existence. The result of the attainment of discrimination is made very much more clear in the *Sūtra* than in the *Kārikā:* the fate of spirit is existence, but entirely without consciousness, as follows inevitably from the fact that there is now no object for the subject to become united with. Moreover, the idea that such a state is one of bliss is properly and logically in accordance with the *Kārikā* expressly rejected, as against the Vedānta theory.

On the means of proof the later text gives little new light: the appeal to the evidence of scripture is far more frequent than might be expected in a system which lays such great stress on reasoning, but this appeal is accepted in the *Kārikā*, and there is not the slightest reason to assume* that the term Āptavacana, which is the normal designation of this branch of proof, ever meant merely skilled instruction. But a real advance is made on the *Kārikā* in the assigning of a definite character to space and time, which are made to be qualities of nature regarded as a unity, and to be eternal and all-present. In the empiric world both appear as limited, and are explained in a quite inconsistent way by origination from the ether through its conditioning by the masses of corporeal nature, on the one hand, in the case of space, and by the movement of the heavenly bodies in the case of time. The first conception is no doubt superior to that of the Vedānta, which produces space from the Ātman, but it is not much superior to the view of the Nyāya and Vaiśeṣika, which call space and time substances,† nor in any of the cases is the real problem of either space or time seriously faced or realized.

The *Sūtra* also includes many points which the *Kārikā* leaves out as unessential. It deals doubtfully with the old question of works as opposed to knowledge and is inconsistent, in one place allowing them value while in others the more consistent view of their total valuelessness comes out, a fact which accords with the lack of any ethical side to the Sāṁkhya system. The necessity of a teacher is laid down, and the only true teacher is one who has attained the saving discrimination in the period before his final release in death: the winning of such a teacher is the result

* See Garbe, *Sāṁkhya Philosophie*, pp. 59, 60.

† Cf. Frazer, *Indian Thought*, pp. 97, 98.

of good deeds in previous lives. A real furtherance, but not a means to secure release, is indifference, Vairāgya, which, again, is a motive for refraining from doing good deeds, with which it is incompatible: moreover, the same quality is definitely opposed to a man's association with other men, which is a hindrance to the desired end. Indifference is divided into the higher which arises only after the attainment of discrimination, and the lower which precedes it: if the latter is carried to its furthest limit, the result is birth as a god in the next world period, pending which the person is merged in nature. Mere hearing of the teaching of the truth is not enough: it must be accompanied by reflection and meditation, and in a marked degree, in contrast to the earlier *Kārikā*, the *Sūtra* adopts large masses of the Yoga technique as a means of producing the desired isolation of spirit and nature. Moreover, the *Sūtra* also accepts from the Yoga the doctrine of the high value of asceticism and the Yogin's power to see all things future and past, a power which is consistent with the Sāṁkhya doctrine of the reality of the product in the cause.

It is characteristic of the Sāṁkhya that it does not restrict, like the Vedānta, the saving knowledge to the three upper classes of the Aryan community to the exclusion of the Śūdras. This generosity of outlook is seen already in the great epic (xiv, 19, 61), where the result of Yoga is distinctly declared to be open even to women and to Śūdras, and the same sentiment can doubtless legitimately be recognized in the fact that the system, despite its fondness for sub-divisions, actually classes in its theory of the kinds of living creatures men in one division only, while divine beings fall under no less than eight. The motive for the difference of treatment doubtless lies in the fact that the Sāṁkhya, like the Yoga, does not build on the Veda as an exclusive foundation, and therefore, unlike the Vedānta, they do not fall under the rule which excludes Śūdras from even hearing the Veda recited. The fact that the Veda formed one of the sources of proof of the system was not any more inconsistent with the system being made available to all, than the fact that the epic which contains Vedic quotations was equally open to Śūdras to hear.

The tendency to obliterate the differences between the Sāṁkhya and the more orthodox philosophies appears in the most pronounced form in the commentary of Vijñānabhikṣu on the *Sāṁkhya Sūtra*, which was probably written about the middle of the sixteenth century A.D. Vijñānabhikṣu, as is seen also in his other works, was convinced that all the six orthodox systems of philosophy contained the absolute truth in their main principles. This paradoxical result is achieved by holding that the Nyāya and the Vaiśeṣika systems are true in so far as they treat of the difference between the self and the material body, but that in attributing agency to the self they merely use popular terminology, which is corrected in the Sāṁkhya system. That system is in appearance atheistic, but Vijñānabhikṣu explains this difficulty away in various modes. The atheism of the Sāṁkhya is in his view merely a concession to current phraseology, or again it is advocated in order to prevent men failing to obtain true enlightenment by devotion to the ideal of attaining divine rank, or again, as suggested in the *Padma Purāṇa*, the doctrine is expressed in order to mislead evil men and prevent their attaining the true knowledge. After this achievement, it is easy for Vijñānabhikṣu to overcome the difficulty that the Vedānta teaches the non-existence of individual souls, and the doctrine of the unity of the absolute, while the Sāṁkhya believes in innumerable individual souls and denies an absolute. The unity of souls of the Vedānta is resolved into a denial of difference in kind, and the monism of scripture is either attributed as a view for the mind devoid of the discriminative understanding, or is asserted merely to mean the absence of separation in space of the souls and matter, which accords with the Sāṁkhya view that souls and matter are alike all-pervasive. Similarly, the assertion of the Vedānta that nature is not real, as in the Sāṁkhya, but a mere illusion, is explained away by the adoption of the view that the Māyā of the Vedānta is really equivalent to the matter of the Sāṁkhya. While in these views of the Vedānta Vijñānabhikṣu is following in the main the original sense of the *Brahma Sūtra* it is perfectly clear that his treatment of the Sāṁkhya is radically in contradiction with the atheism of that system, which is set out with arguments in the very text (v, 2-11) which he professes to expound.

The attitude adopted by Vijñānabhikṣu is significant of the theistic spirit of his age: in his exposition the six systems present themselves as nothing but a theistic exposition of the universe, presented less directly in the four systems of the Nyāya and Vaiśeṣika, Sāṁkhya and Yoga, and brought out in the clearest manner in the Vedānta. By this device the Sāṁkhya philosophy is brought into the main current of Indian thought and relieved from the disadvantages of its atheism, which doubtless accounts for the comparative disfavour in which the Sāṁkhya system had long fallen in India, and to which Vijñānabhikṣu himself bears emphatic testimony.

While the attempt of Vijñānabhikṣu could not expect to result in the establishment of the authority of the Sāṁkhya as a system, the influence of that philosophy may doubtless be traced directly in the free admission of elements of the Sāṁkhya into the texts of the later Vedānta. This interfusion of Vedānta and Sāṁkhya elements is seen in the *Bhagavadgītā*, but the doctrine of Guṇas was distinctly repudiated by Śaṁkara, and its reappearance in texts, which accept his general principles and believe in the illusory character of the world, is a clear proof that the reasoning of the Sāṁkhya was felt to have great weight. Of this syncretist tendency, which is seen clearly in the *Pañcadaśī* of Mādhava in the fourteenth century A.D., the classical example is to be found in the *Vedāntasāra* of Sadānanda, a work written before 1500 A.D. Sadānanda identifies, as in the *Svetāśvatara Upaniṣad*, the Māyā, or Avidyā, of the Vedānta with the Prakṛti of the Sāṁkhya, and by accepting the view that Prakṛti is composed of three elements obtains the means of fitting much of the Sāṁkhya system into the Vedānta. From Brahman, who is regarded by him as essentially Caitanya, or spirit, is produced through envelopment with ignorance in its constituent of Sattva the world-spirit, Īśvara, whose causal body out of which he creates all things is composed by the whole of ignorance. On the other hand, from the Caitanya through envelopment with Sattva in an impure form, that is mixed with the constituents, Rajas and Tamas, arises the individual spirit, Prājña, which has as its causal body out of which it creates individuation, etc., and is composed of only a part of ignorance. A further result of envelopment is the creation of the world soul, Sūtrātman, and the individual soul, Taijasa, from the world-spirit and the individual spirit, by the production, through the effect of the constituent Tamas, of the fine body. From the Caitanya enveloped by ignorance through the predominance of Tamas arises the ether, from the ether, wind; from wind, fire; from fire, water; and from water, earth. In each of these elements, however, which are only in a fine state, there is a portion of the constituents Rajas and Sattva as well as of Tamas. From these five Tanmātras arise the fine body, consisting of five organs of perception produced from the Sattva portions of the corresponding five elements, of five organs of action arising from the Rajas portions of the elements, of intelligence and mind consisting of united portions of Sattva from the elements, and of the five breaths, consisting of united portions of Rajas from the five elements. In intelligence and mind spirit, Citta, and individuation are held to be included, and in this respect, as in the giving of an independent position to the five breaths, the Sāṁkhya doctrine is abandoned. Similarly, in the view of the production of the elements from each other in a series, Sadānanda follows the *Taittirīya Upaniṣad* (ii, 1) and not the Sāṁkhya. On the other hand, the development of the gross world body and the individual body, Vaiśvānara and Viśva, takes place according to the Sāṁkhya rule of five elements, not according to the Vedānta rule of three.

At the same time it must be noted that the influence of the Sāṁkhya is clearly limited in extent: the whole system of four states, Brahman, Īśvara and Prājña, Sūtrātman and Taijasa, Vaiśvānara and Viśva, is based on the Vedānta view of the four conditions of the self, in its conditions of freedom from bondage, deep sleep, dreaming, and waking, respectively, as set out in the *Bṛhadāraṇyaka Upaniṣad* (iv, 3-4), the *Māṇḍūkya Upaniṣad* (3-5), and in a developed form in the *Nṛsiṁhottaratāpanīya Upaniṣad*. It is, however, possible that in the care taken to insist on the cosmic character of the process, which in the earlier Upaniṣads is expressly restricted to the states of the individual souls, there may be seen the influence of the Sāṁkhya, with its insistence on the cosmic character of the development of Prakṛti, and, despite the constant variation of detail, the importance of the Guṇas in the system is obvious.

While the interaction of Vedānta and Sāṁkhya is thus marked, there are few traces of close connection with the Nyāya school. The most important is the exposition of the doctrine of inference found in Vācaspatimiśra's commentary on *Sāṁkhya Kārikā* 5, which appears to mark an independent development by the Sāṁkhya of principles adopted, more or less uncritically in the first instance, from the Nyāya rather than to contain a record of a doctrine presupposed by the early form of Sāṁkhya.* In this view inference is divided into direct (*vīta*) and indirect (*avīta*); the latter category coincides with *śeṣavat*, and means proof by the elimination of alternative explanations; the former includes *pūrvavat* and *sāmānyato dṛṣṭa*, which differ in that the result of the former is a judgment dealing with realities which can be perceived, while the latter gives knowledge of such imperceptible entities as the senses or the soul.

* As suggested by A Bürk, *Vienna Oriental Journal*, XV, 259, 261.

INDEX

ABHIBUDDHI 90
Abhimāna 35, 36
Aboriginal influence 16, 54
Absolute, see Brahman
Adṛṣṭa 24
Ages of the World 19, 96
Ahaṁkāra 18, 24, 35, 36, 78-80, 95
Ahiṁsā 47, 50, 71
Ahirbudhnya Saṁhitā 60, 61
Aitareya Āraṇyaka 16
Aniruddha 33, 35
Aniruddha, commentator 92
Anugītā 29, 31, 32, 34, 36
Ānu-śrāvika 61, 62
Anuyogadvāra Sūtra 60
Ānvīkṣikī 47, 58
Arāḍa 22, 23
Aśakti 62, 84, 90
Asambhūti 18
Asaṅga 20, 57
Asceticism 100
Asiddhi 62, 84, 90
Asita Devala 40
Asmitā 84
Āsuri 39, 41, 42
Aśvaghoṣa 22, 23
Atharvaveda 19, 48
Atheism 20, 28, 47, 93, 101, 102
Ātivāhika body 97
Ātman 3, 6, 17, 48
Atomic size, of spirit 43; of mind 93
Atoms 57, 93
Atuṣṭi 90
Aupapātika Sūtra 60
Avidyā 23-25, 84, 87, 88, 98
Aviśeṣa 47, 97
Avyakta 9, 73, 74, and see Nature

BĀDARĀYAṆA 6, 7, 52
Bala 36, 39
Beasts 34, 98
Belvarkar, S. K. 62*n*, 64*n*, 68*n*, 70*n*
Bhagavadgītā 29, 31, 33, 56, 102
Bhāgavatas 33, 35, 49
Bhāvas 10, 59, 60, 83, 84
Bhoga 61
Bhūtas 13
Bhūtādi 90
Bhūtātman 33, 36
Brahman, the 5, 6, 13, 31, 49, 56
Brahman (masc.) 31, 38, 45, 56, 61, 83, 102
Brahma Sūtra 6, 52
Brahmavidyā 47
Brāhmaṇas, doctrines of 6, 7, 16, 48
Breath, see Prāṇa
Bṛhadāraṇyaka Upaniṣad 6, 8, 16, 17, 18, 31, 48, 52, 76, 103
Buddhacarita 22
Buddhi 36, 87-81, 95
Buddhīndriyas 36, 78, 80
Buddhism 13, 17, 18, 20-28, 44, 71, 92
Bürk, A. 72*n*, 104*n*

CAITANYA 102
Cārvākas 71, 92
Causal series, in Buddhism 22, 23
Causality, doctrine of 73, 93
Chāndogya Upaniṣad 6, 9, 16, 18, 48, 81
Charpentier, J. 57*n*, 58*n*
Chinese tradition 41, 59
Christianity, possible influence of 29, 30
Citta 35
Cosmology 6, 31, 45
Connection between spirit and matter 42, 78, 85-88
Cūlikā Upaniṣad 19

DAHLMANN, J. 47-49
Deities presiding over the senses 90
Deussen, P. 5*n*, 9*n*, 13*n*, 25, 55, 71, 79*n*
Dharma 61
Dharmâdharmau 24
Dreams 36
Dṛṣṭi 61
Dveṣa 85

EGG, cosmic 18, 31, 45
Eight, sets of 35
Elements, see Mahâbhūta and Tanmātra
Eschatology 38, 86, 98, 99
Ether 67
Ethics 37, 38, 99, 100

FINE elements, see Tanmātra
Flower, with nine doors 19, 48
Form 23, 24, 25
Four stages of self 103

GARBE, R. 30*n*, 43, 46, 49, 54*n*, 59, 66, 77*n*, 79*n*, 95, 99*n*
Garbha Upaniṣad 19
Garga 39, 44
Gauḍapāda 67, 82, 83
Gnosticism 66
Gods 83, 97; proof of existence of 72; and see Īśvara
Gough, A. E. 12*n*, 16*n*, 54*n*, 95*n*
Greek Philosophy 65-67
Gross body 44, 97, 98; elements, see Mahābhūtas
Guṇa 61
Guṇas 10, 11, 13, 19, 34, 45, 46, 48, 51, 78, 90, 96, 102

HELL 38
Hiraṇyagarbha 8, 39, 79
Hophins, E. W. 34*n*, 37*n*, 49
Hypostatization of one aspect of consciousness 76, 77

IGNORANCE 23-25, 42, 87, 88, 98
Illusion, doctrine of 6, 7, 20, 28, 31, 48, 101
Indifference 100
Individuation, see Ahaṁkāra.
Inference 71, 72, 104
Infinite size, of inner organ 57; of spirit 43
Inner organ 57, 81, 94, 95
Intellect, see Buddhi
Īśā Upaniṣad 18
Īśvara 33, 38, 56, 102
Īśvarakṛṣṇa 43, 57, 63

JACOBI, H. 6*n*, 19*n*, 22, 30*n*, 43
Jaigīṣavya 39, 44
Jains 92
Jevons, F. B. 77*n*
Jīva 37, 98

KAPILA 8, 12, 39, 40, 42, 47, 50
Kapilavastu 50
Karmendriyas 36, 78, 80
Kartṛ 61
Kaṣāya 60
Kaṭha Upaniṣad 8, 9, 15, 16, 18*n*, 36, 46, 51, 55, 78, 98*n*
Kauṣītaki (or *Śāṅkhāyana*) *Brāhmaṇa* 16, 48
Kauṣītaki Upaniṣad 8, 16, 88*n*, 95
Kauṭilya Arthaśāstra 58
Kāvila 60
Khyāti 61
Kleśa 61
Knowledge, as source of release 15, 23-25, 87, 88, 98
Kṛṣṇa 34
Kṛtya Kāṇḍa 61
Kṣatriyas, and philosophy 49, 50
Kṣetrajña 32, 35
Kūrma Purāṇa 44
Kutsāyana 14

LANMAN, C. R. 19*n*
Lévi, S. 16*n*
Liṅga 18, 36, 82
Lokāyata 68

MĀDHAVA 91, 102
Mādhyamikas 93
Mahābhārata, and Sāṁkhya 29-53

Mahābhūtas 13, 78, 81-83, 95, 97
Mahāmoha 84
Mahān, see Buddhi
Maitrāyaṇī Upaniṣad 8, 12, 13, 14, 17, 18*n*, 55
Māṇḍūkya Upaniṣad 103
Manu 14, 44, 45
Mātāpitṛjas 83
Materialists 18, 71, 92
Māṭhara-Vṛtti 68*n*, 70*n*
Mātrā 10, and see Tanmātra
Matsya Purāṇa 46
Matter 6-8, 18, 31, 47, 52, 77-79
Max Müller, F. 5*n*, 13*n*, 68, 77, 89
Māyā 6, 7, 20, 31, 48, 101, 102
Memory 81
Mind 36, 79, 80
Mirror, metaphor of 94
Mokṣa 27, 38, 62, 85-87, 91, 96-98
Mokṣadharma 29
Monad, individual as 83
Mūlikārthas 60, 91
Multiplicity, of souls 52, 77, 78, 87, 101
Muṇḍaka Upaniṣad 14, 15, 88*n*
Muni, mad 54
Mysticism 55

NĀGĀRJUNA 20
Nāgeśa Bhaṭṭa 92
Name 23, 24, 25
Nārāyaṇatīrtha 60, 70
Nature 31, 43, 47, 52, 77-79
Neoplatonism and Sāṁkhya, 67
Nervous system 95
Nihilism 20
Niranumāna 90
Nirvāṇa 26, 38, 47
Nṛsiṁhatāpanīya Upaniṣad 19
Nyāya, school 93, 97, 99, 101
Nyāya Darśana 93

OLDENBERG, H. 5*n*, 9*n*, 22, 24, 25
Oltramare, P. 16*n*, 19*n*, 25
Organs, of action 36, 78, 80

PADMA PURĀṆA 101
Pāñcarātra 50, 60
Pañcaśikha 39, 41, 42, 62, 97
Paramārtha 59
Pāśupata 45, 49, 50, 60
Patañjali 30, 54, 56, 57
Perception 71
Pessimism 13, 15, 16, 17, 71, 91
Plants 34, 98
Plato 17, 67
Pradyumna 33, 35
Prajāpati 83
Prājña 103
Prakṛti 18, 46, 59, 77, 102, and see Nature
Pramāṇas 45, 61, 71, 72, 99
Prāṇa 15, 37, 61, 80, 90, 98, 103
Praśna Upaniṣad 9
Priests, hostility to sacrificial 71
Punarmṛtyu 16, 17
Purāṇas 18, 45, 46
Puruṣa 11, 31, 32, 61, 74, 75-88, 98-100
Pūrva Mīmāṁsā 28
Pythagoras 17, 66

RĀGA 85
Rājendralāla Mitra 55*n*
Rakṣases 83
Rājavārttika 59
Rājas 12, 14, 34, 74, 78, 79, 80, 103
Rebirth 38, and see Transmigration.
Release, from transmigration, see Mokṣa
Retaḥśarīra 36
Ṛgveda 8, 16, 19, 48, 54
Ṛudra 10

ŚABARASVĀMIN 43
Sadānanda 102
Śakti 43, 61
Samavāya 93
Śaṁkara 6, 7, 18, 20, 48, 88, 92, 93, 94, 95*n*, 102
Saṁkarṣaṇa 33, 35
Saṁkhājogī 60
Sāṁkhya Kārikā 21, 41, 51, 62, 68-78
Sāṁkhya Sūtra 41, 44, 92-100
Saṁskāras 23, 24, 86, 95

Sana 44
Sanaka 44
Sanandana 42
Sanātana 44
Sanatkumāra 39, 41, 44
Sanatsujāta 44
Sanatsujātīya 29
Sānumāna 90
Sarvadarśanasaṁgraha 92
Ṣaṣṭitantra 41, 59-64
Śatapatha Brāhmaṇa 16, 17, 48
Sattva 12, 14, 18, 34, 74, 78, 79, 80, 102, 103
Sāttvika 34
Sātvata 60
Sautrāntika school 57
Schrader, F. O. 16*n*, 40*n*
Schroeder, L. v. 66
Scripture, as means of proof 51, 72, 99
Self consciousness 94, 95
Senses 80, 97
Siddhi, 62, 84, 90
Simile of blind and lame 76; of dancer 85, 86; of lamp 74; of mirror 94, of she-goat 11
Śiva 10, 46
Soul, activity of denied 93, and see Ātman, Jīva, Puruṣa
Sound, see Sphoṭa
Space 43, 99
Speyer, J. S. 49*n*
Spirit, 23, 31, 32, 38, 61, 74-88, 98-100
Sphoṭa 57, 61, 94
Śruti, see Scripture
Svayambhū 45
Śvetāśvatara Upaniṣad 8, 10, 11, 12, 13, 18*n*, 30, 39, 46, 51, 55, 102
Strauss, O. 36*n*
Subtle portions, of gross elements 82, 83, 97
Śūdras 100
Sukhtankar 6
Sūtrātman 163
Svāmin 61

TAIJASA 90
Taittirīya, Upaniṣad 37, 82, 103
Takakusu 63*n*, 69
Tamas 12, 14, 34, 74, 78, 80, 103
Tāmisra 84
Tanmātra 10, 13, 37, 78, 81, 95, 97, 103
Tattvasamāsa 61, 68, 89-92
Teacher, necessity of a 99, 100
Tejas 6
Theism 7, 8, 30, 31, 47, 56, 61
Thibaut, G. 6*n*
Time 57, 61, 99
Traditional rules, value of 94
Transmigration 15, 16, 38, 71, 83, 84
Tuṣṭi 62, 84, 85, 90
Tuxen, P. 55*n*, 56*n*, 57*n*, 63*n*
Twenty-five principles 32, 48, 78
Twenty-six principles 32, 55

ULŪKA (?) 44
Upādāna 24
Upādhi 98
Upaniṣads 5-19, 87
Uvaṭa 14

VĀCASPATI 42, 59, 62, 70' 80*n*
Vaikārika 34, 90
Vairāgya 61, 100
Vaiśeṣika system 57, 93, 97, 99, 101
Vaiṣṇava 46
Vaiśvānara 103
Varṣagaṇa, or Vṛṣagaṇa 63
Vārṣagaṇya 39, 62, 63
Vasubandhu 57, 68
Vāsudeva 33
Vedānta 20, 37, 43, 45, 78, 80, 82, 87, 90, 97, 98, 100, 101, 102
Vijñāna 23-25, 89
Vijñānabhikṣu 57, 72*n*, 101
Vijñānātman 10, 11
Vijñānavāda 28, 57, 93
Vikṛti 61
Vindhyavāsa 62, 68
Viparyaya 62, 84
Viśeṣa 37, 47
Viśiṣṭādvaita 6, 22
Viṣṇu, 46
Viṣṇu Purāṇa 46

Viṣṇu Smṛti 45
Viśva 103
Voḍhu 44
Vyāmiśra 36
Vyāpti 43
Vyāsa 42, 57
Vyūha 33

WALLESER, M. 25*n*
Way, of the gods and fathers 38
Weber, A. 41*n*
Whitney, W. D. 19*n*
Women 100
Woods, J. H. 43*n*
Works 99
World, periodic destruction of 19, 96

YĀJÑAVALKYA 5, 16, 52, 77
Yakṣas 83
Yoga 23, 33, 38, 49, 50, 54-58, 60, 94, 100
Yoga Sūtra 30, 54
Yogin, powers of 97, 100